THE LAST
BEST HOPE

THE LAST
BEST HOPE

A History of
American Realism

DR. JOHN HULSMAN

First published 2024 by John Hulsman,
in partnership with Whitefox Publishing Ltd.

www.wearewhitefox.com

ISBN 9781915635648

Also available as an eBook
ISBN 9781915635655

Also available as an audiobook
ISBN 9781915635969

Designed and typeset by seagulls.net
Cover design by Dan Mogford
Project management by Whitefox
Printed and bound by Marquis, Canada

This book is dedicated to Sara,

who is the beginning and the ending of everything for me.

"We shall nobly save, or meanly lose, the last best hope of earth."

Abraham Lincoln, Message to Congress, December 1862

CONTENTS

INTRODUCTION

Saving the last best hope

It was the worst possible time to begin a social revolution. December 1862 was the zenith of the year of miracles for the southern Confederacy. From June 1862—when, following the severe wounding of General Joseph E. Johnston, Robert E. Lee assumed command of the Army of Northern Virginia—until June 1863, on the cusp of the Battle of Gettysburg, the South could do almost no wrong.

Lee outgeneraled George McClellan during the Seven Days Battles of June–July 1862, then demolished John Pope at the Second Battle of Manassas in August 1862. Next, and perhaps most amazingly, even when the North had the great good fortune of knowing every detail of Lee's planned invasion of Maryland (which was discovered in three unburned cigar wrappers), the South somehow managed a tactical draw against the briefly reinstated McClellan at the Battle of Antietam on September 17, 1862, the bloodiest single day's fighting of the war.

Before the tide was turned at Gettysburg in early July 1863, the southern year of miracles added dominant victories at Fredericksburg (December 1862) and Lee's masterpiece, Chancellorsville, in April–May 1863. As a direct result of the North's failure to quickly put down the rebellion, the 1862 midterm elections had not gone well for Lincoln's Republican Party, which had sustained losses of 22 seats in the House (despite maintaining a plurality) while the opposition Democrats gained 28.[1] No, in the midst of all this military failure, it was not a propitious time for beleaguered President Abraham Lincoln to embark on a fundamental remodeling of the country's basic social structure, by beginning to do away with the evil of slavery.

Yet Lincoln persevered nonetheless. While it was dispiriting that the South had somehow managed a tactical draw at Antietam, Lee had been forced to retreat to his Virginia stronghold following the carnage, amounting to a strategic victory for the North. The president seized upon this rare piece of good news, amidst a year of disasters, to go ahead with the most daring policy initiative that had been attempted in America since the founding of the nation in the 1780s—the emancipation of the 4 million slaves held in southern territory.

A month before signing the Emancipation Proclamation, on December 1, 1862, in fulfillment of his constitutional duties (Article II, Section 3), Lincoln sent his second annual message to Congress,[2] then delivered in written form.* While the vast majority of it reads like a mind-numbing laundry list of what the federal government was doing at the time—establishing a Department of Agriculture, managing America's finances, inaugurating a continental railway system, dealing with warring Native Americans—at the end Lincoln abruptly and majestically shifted gear, urging Congress to lift up its eyes and to think far ahead, about the future of the Union after the conclusion of the Civil War.

In September 1862, following Antietam, Lincoln had warned his Cabinet that he planned to abolish slavery in the southern-held territories by Executive Order, as a war measure, by January 1, 1863. Washington, then as now, was a perpetual hotbed of gossip, so the coming proclamation was by December the worst-kept secret in the Capitol.

The end of his second annual message to the Congress was Lincoln paving the way for the coming proclamation. Linking the abolition of

---

* While Washington had delivered the message as a speech, Jefferson had discontinued the practice, considering the format too monarchical. Between his time and the modern era, the message was delivered in written form, as Lincoln dutifully complied with in December 1862. It was only in the early twentieth century that Woodrow Wilson went back to the original practice of delivering the State of the Union as a speech in front of both houses of Congress.

slavery to the future of the country itself, he boldly stated, "In giving freedom to the slave, we assure freedom to the free."[3] Crucially, in one of the text's few mentions of foreign affairs, the president was explicitly clear that the US left "to every nation the exclusive conduct and management of its own affairs."[4] America was far too busy trying to salvage its own experiment with democratic governance to arrogantly tell other countries what to do.

But the president had saved the best of his oratory for last. Echoing Jefferson's first inaugural, in which he had called America "the world's best hope,"[5] Lincoln ringingly ended, in reference to the planned emancipation, "We shall nobly save, or meanly lose, the last best hope of earth."[6]

These words have resonated with the American people down the ages because they so fundamentally track with how Americans feel about themselves, their place in the world, and the country they have forged. America's sense of itself has always included huge dollops of both fear and hope—that the republic and the experiment in democratic governance are beset by endless peril, while at the same time the promise of the American Revolution remains the universal hope of man. Ironically, just as Lincoln went back to Jefferson to find a way forward for a post-Civil War America, we must now go back in time to him, to find a way forward for our country as it enters our new, present Age of Insecurity.

The Jacksonians

The purpose of this work is as beguilingly simple as it is forthrightly ambitious. This book will serve as a clarion call for a new dominant realist foreign policy alliance within conservative circles, fusing the populist Jacksonian base of the GOP with the more libertarian Jeffersonian school of thought.

Rather than reinventing the wheel, we will draw on the never-bettered US foreign policy typologies put forward by Walter Russell

Mead in his masterpiece, *Special Providence: American Foreign Policy and How It Changed the World.*[7] Mead's particular genius, beyond shrewdly detailing the major American foreign policy schools of thought belief systems, is to organically imprint each with an American historical figure who most epitomizes what each school of thought is actually about.

For the purposes of our book (though I strongly advise you to read the whole of Mead's groundbreaking work), we will ignore the left-leaning, Democratic Party-based Hamiltonians and Wilsonians. Now that Donald Trump has usefully exiled the shoot-first-and-ask-questions-later neoconservatives to their proper home in a Democratic Party that is all about social engineering, we will instead be focusing on the two major foreign policy strands currently dominating the Republican Party.

These two conservative foreign policy schools of thought are surely not the same. Jeffersonians like Johnny Cash; Jacksonians are Johnny Cash. Jeffersonians adore the First Amendment; Jacksonians are passionate about the Second. Jeffersonians support the FIRE; Jacksonians the NRA.* Jeffersonians support populism, but much like their namesake, from an elitist perch; Jacksonians are truly of the people. Beyond these social and cultural differences, over policy the two tend to divide over free trade, with Jeffersonians being enthusiastic supporters while Jacksonians are inherently more protectionist.

But for all these differences, there is more that unites these two schools of thought than divides them. Above all, they are fused together by a common (if unacknowledged) adherence to realism, which can and must serve as the cement for the new, dominant foreign policy orientation of the Republican Party. With neoconservatives fleeing conservative circles with the advent of Donald Trump and with neoconservatism increasingly

---

* Respectively, the Foundation for Individual Rights and Expression, and the National Rifle Association.

discredited in general, the GOP can at last shake off the stigma of failed promiscuous interventions in wars of choice such as the debacle in Iraq, and futile nation-building exercises such as America's two-decade disaster in Afghanistan. There has never been a better time for the re-ascendance of realist principles in conservative circles.

Specifically, Jacksonians share with Jeffersonians a suspicion of unfettered federal government power, preferring such government as is necessary to reside closest to the people; that is, with the states and localities. Their common ancestors doubtless carried the famous serpent flag of the Revolutionary War, "Don't Tread on Me," as both schools are fearsome defenders of individual liberty. Originally, in line with their formidable namesake, Andrew Jackson, Jacksonians were pre-revolutionary Scots-Irish settlers, who quickly moved as far away as possible from coastal control, inhabiting the Old West of West Virginia, Ohio, Kentucky, Illinois, Indiana, and parts of the South.

In terms of social policy, Jacksonians believe self-reliance is a core value, that every individual has equal rights, but differing life outcomes are to be expected. They believe in both the dignity of the country and the dignity of the individual. Jacksonians, like their dueling namesake, believe America is an honor culture, whose prerogatives must be fought for, if necessary.

Jacksonians absolutely hate today's leftist woke movement, both because they despise its self-loathing and deprecation of an America they love and because they believe that absolutely no one has the right to tell a self-reliant Jacksonian what to say, what to think, or what to do. The same holds true for the United States in general, as in this honor culture the US must not submit itself to lectures from unelected foreign technocrats of any kind. The American government's role is to provide for the well-being of this folk community. The American people do not need to be educated (let alone socially engineered) by the country's coastal elites, and especially not by arrogant foreigners.

As such, both Jacksonians and Jeffersonians fear rule from far away, being particularly suspicious of globalist do-gooding by unelected foreigner-run international institutions, such as the United Nations (UN) and International Criminal Court (ICC), as well as international agreements which bind Americans, such as the green Kyoto Protocol. Jacksonians are realists on this key plank, wanting no international institution or treaty to constrain America's freedom of maneuver.

Part of the reason for this reluctance for America to be bound stems from the fact that the Jacksonian honor culture means that the US has a sworn obligation to protect those it has actually given its word to. As such, interventions and conventions should not be entered into lightly. For example, over Vietnam, Jacksonians were the last school of thought to get excited about the war, given that primary American interests did not seem to be at stake. However, once the US was committed, Jacksonians were also the last foreign policy group to want to leave, given that America had given South Vietnam its word to fight shoulder to shoulder with Saigon.

For Jacksonians, there should be no such thing as a limited war. Either America is fully committed or it simply should not be militarily involved. Either the stakes are important enough for the US to fight for—in which case you should commit to total war—or they are not and you should stay home. As such, Jacksonians resent any effort to stop short of victory.

For all these reasons, Jacksonians are staunchly opposed to recent Humanitarian Interventions in places like Somalia, Haiti, Bosnia, Kosovo and Libya, where there are no significant American interests at play. For Jacksonians, countries—like families—should first and primarily take care of their own.[8]

In line with realist thinking, Jacksonians believe that the international system is anarchic and violent and will remain so forever. America must be ever vigilant and have a strong military always at the ready to defend the country itself. For all this, Jacksonians are not "isolationist," as so many of their simplistic detractors allege. Aggressive when they perceive primary American interests to be at stake, Jacksonians are simply far less so when they perceive they are not, as in the multiple interventions in the 1990s in then-collapsing Yugoslavia.

It was the Jacksonians who formed the crucial core of the Trump revolution which swept aside the old, decrepit GOP establishment. The old elite's cardinal sins were that they did not really care about illegal immigration, spent trillions of dollars on wars not in the primary national interests of the country, focused more on their business friends than on US workers over trade deals, and never attacked woke politics. All of these things made the Bush-era Republicans increasingly suspect in Jacksonian eyes.

To the contrary, Trump assiduously tended to his Jacksonian base, starting no new wars of choice, focusing on law and order, attacking woke-ness in society, promoting government deregulation and tax cuts, and establishing a proactive energy policy based on fracking and increased drilling. Rarely has a politician so kept faith with his core supporters, which explains their fervent loyalty to Trump, come hell or high water, in return. The new political reality, which will last after he eventually leaves the stage, is that the base of the Republican Party will remain solidly Jacksonian and Trumpist well into the future.

The Jeffersonians

The Jeffersonians also make up an important piece of the conservative coalition—one more lodged in elite and decision-making circles than the Jacksonians, if smaller in size overall.[9] They, like the Jacksonians, lack the Wilsonian left's missionary zeal regarding the rest of the world. Both conservative schools of thought would not mind the world becoming more like America, though they think this unlikely to happen. What they are both sure of is that they don't want America becoming more like the rest of the world. Instead, both schools of thought are united in a fervent belief in American exceptionalism—that the specific cultural, social, and political heritage of the United States is a precious gift bequeathed to us by the founders, and not one to be squandered.

Unlike liberal hawks or neoconservatives, for Jeffersonians the basic object of US foreign policy is to defend American values at home rather than to extend them overseas. In particular, they feel building a successful republic in one country is more than enough to keep America busy. Democracy is seen as a fragile plant, difficult to grow and still more difficult to propagate. As such, America's mission in the world is to serve as an example for the virtues of democracy, rather than ignorantly and ruinously attempting to impose it at the point of a gun upon societies of which we know little.

For Jeffersonians, democracy can never be taken for granted; it must be forthrightly defended. Even more than their Jacksonian allies, Jeffersonians believe fervently in the basic fact that the United States is exceptional and different from the rest of the world, and that this uniqueness must be defended at all costs. Jeffersonianism is inherently a defensive creed, with the preservation of the individual liberty made manifest in the American Revolution amounting to the highest aim of statecraft. Liberty may be infinitely precious but Jeffersonians also believe it is infinitely fragile.

These basic views lead Jeffersonians to be concerned with dangers to the domestic tranquility of the country, given excessive entanglements in foreign quarrels. Involvement in overseas wars requires a centralized, high-tax-gathering, bureaucracy-heavy state with an overweening military-industrial complex—all conditions that Jeffersonians rightly fear limit liberty and encourage tyranny, and are fundamentally corrupting of American democracy. As such, Jeffersonians tend to see foreign affairs more through the lens of mitigating threats rather than exploiting opportunities. While isolation cannot be an answer, a restrained foreign policy that limits these domestic dangers to American institutions at the least possible risk and cost is the way ahead.

For Jeffersonians, then, war is to be avoided at almost all costs, being the last resort of foreign policy—rather than the first resort, as neoconservatives advocate—primarily because wars carry with them the seeds to undermine American liberty at home. Today's imperial presidency is the result of the permanent foreign policy crisis that was the Cold War of 1945–91, characterized by the rise and rise of the national security state, excessive secrecy, vast debt, and extraconstitutional, unfettered power for the chief executive.

A basic way to avoid foreign entanglements for Jeffersonians is for the US to recognize that its primary national interests are narrow. They see the risks and costs of intervention as so high that only basic threats to the nation's existence—such as World War II—justify military involvement.

Another reason for this foreign policy restraint is the Jeffersonian's frugality. A dollar not frittered away on social engineering in faraway countries of only peripheral importance to the US means a dollar not taken from American citizens. I have often said at meetings with deadbeat European governments that they don't get to tell me what to do with my army, as I am the only one in the room paying for it, whether I want to or not.

Without a crusading, overly expansive foreign policy, determined to right all the wrongs of the world, there is far less corresponding need for an overweening military-industrial complex. Without such powerful vested interests getting in the way—in terms of lobbying for a vast, unaccountable centralizing government, addicted to war and gobbling up and misspending the patrimony of the country—the riches of America can be returned to where they belong: its enterprising people.

Realism as the glue

As we can see, Jacksonians and Jeffersonians are surely not the same. Yet they are more than similar enough—and together unquestionably have both the intellectual and political heft to dominate the Republican Party far into the future—to form an alliance as the new preeminent foreign policy impulse on the conservative right in the United States. And the glue that unites them, despite their real differences, is realism.

It has often been said, most recently by Emma Ashford in *Foreign Affairs*, that realism is not really a coherent man-made philosophy. More accurately, it is a set of enduring precepts and impulses, grounded in history, that have made sense of the world since the dawn of time.[10]

As Ashford rightly sets out, first, most realists think states are primarily guided by questions of security and survival. Second, states act primarily on the basis of their national interest rather than utopian, universalist principles. Third, the international system, never having had a world government, is defined by anarchy. Fourth, realist foreign policy initiatives are defined by pragmatism, the art of the possible, rather than grand and doomed otherworldly ideological crusades. Fifth, whereas the Wilsonians who dominate the Democratic Party believe that (somehow) states can rise above conflict and power politics—whether through the magic of trade, international institutions, or international law—all realists categorically reject that such a transcendence is possible. Sixth, and finally, because of this basic state of the world, most realists emphasize prudence as a policy-making virtue beyond all others.

This general depiction of realism takes us a long way down the road toward a fundamental Jacksonian-Jeffersonian intellectual and political alliance, as both major US foreign policy schools of thought can effortlessly (unlike their Wilsonian and Hamiltonian rivals) get behind these basic realist precepts. But if this is generally what realism is about, there needs to be another layer of specificity to the grand Jacksonian-Jeffersonian bargain: how have realist impulses played out in America's own history as it has actually been lived?

For using applied history—looking at the specific history of American realism to find the basic organic building blocks for the future of this grand conservative alliance—is what this book is all about. As Lincoln did with Jefferson, so we must now also do with our common American past, mining it to see who we are, what this means, and how this common realist past can animate the Jacksonian-Jeffersonian future.

A history of American realism

This book will consist of nine vignettes drawn from US history, mining basic realist precepts gleaned from the American story that serve as the foreign policy basis for the coming Jacksonian-Jeffersonian accord. The conclusion of this book will take the nine precepts of this applied history and convert them into a practical American realist foreign policy for today, using them as compass points to navigate the new geostrategic world we actually find ourselves in. Politically, these nine precepts and conclusion must rally today's Jacksonians and Jeffersonians around a common positive vision of conservative realism, fit for purpose in our new age.

Employing storytelling from the American saga, we will create a positive vision for conservative realism that will fuse the Jacksonians and Jeffersonians together. Through this political marriage, it is to be hoped that this book will have a profound impact on the intellectual direction of foreign policy decision-making in the GOP for years to come. There has never been a greater opportunity to reclaim the primacy of realism and restraint in terms of conservative thought. This book hopes to grasp it.

The nine precepts of American realism

1. **Alliances should only be entered into when they advance specific and primary American interests.** We will look at the fraught circumstances surrounding the Jay Treaty and Washington's Farewell Address as the template for the country's astounding foreign policy success of its first 100 years.

2. **"No more stupid wars."** Fighting wars of choice, from Humanitarian Interventions on the Wilsonian left (recently Haiti, Bosnia, Kosovo, and Somalia and Libya) to nation-building exercises on the neoconservative right (recently Iraq and Afghanistan), is ruinous to America's overall position in the world. American military power must be husbanded for use only when primary American national interests are at stake. To make this case, we will look at the long and distinguished career of John Quincy Adams, who led the charge in opposing promiscuous interventions.

3. **To act, or not to act, depends on the national interest.** Compared with today's foreign policy blob, which tends to do far too much far too badly, the US must be more discerning—being aggressive (diplomatically, economically, and even militarily) when its primary national interests are at stake, and far less so when they are not. We will look at how Abraham Lincoln's Secretary of State, William H. Seward, adroitly avoided an unnecessary war with Victorian England while prosecuting an absolutely vital war with the Confederacy.

4. **Sovereignty is real and everything.** Be the issue managing America's borders, energy independence, or not outsourcing US decision-making to unaccountable international institutions, America must preserve its freedom to act on its own as it chooses to in the world. We will examine the underrated Senator William Borah's successful opposition to Woodrow Wilson's League of Nations.

5. **America must never shirk using force to fight wars when its primary interests are at stake, but it must also never go abroad looking for a fight over lesser interests.** There is a difference between a Hitler and a Milosevic. We will follow the story of how, over time, FDR masterfully prepared the US for World War II.

6. **Furthering the immediate and specific interests of the American people must be the never-forgotten touchstone**

of any successful US foreign policy. We will look in detail at Eisenhower's warning about a military-industrial complex, a permanent war party, seeing in today's foreign policy blob an establishment which often cares more about the sufferings of others than the real calamities befalling our own people.

7. **Above all, American national interests (designed to secure the American nation) should always drive US foreign policy.** We will dissect JFK's handling of the Cuban Missile Crisis, where he threaded the needle, forcing the Soviets to back down (securing primary US interests) while at the same time avoiding the apocalypse of nuclear war.

8. **The US must be ruthlessly prepared to cut deals with the devil, coming to terms with less than savory countries if doing so furthers US interests.** We will look at Nixon's masterstroke in going to China, mightily contributing to overall victory in the Cold War.

9. **The US must be a "shining city on a hill," and not be in the foolhardy business of trying to impose democracy upon the rest of the world.** We will end our history of American realism by examining the wildly successful career of Ronald Reagan, who understood better than anyone that America-as-example is a great source of its power.

In conclusion, we will put all these organic precepts gleaned from applied history to work, using the new Jacksonian-Jeffersonian fusion around American realism to look at the world of today, devising a coherent, overall foreign policy that flows from this new, yet old, way of looking at the world. The compelling imperative of this book is as ambitious as it is necessary. For if we can change the Republican Party, we can change America; and if we can change America, we can change the world. It is as simple, and as important, as this.

~ 1 ~

WASHINGTON SETS
US ON OUR WAY

*"Alliances should only be entered
into when they advance specific and
primary American interests"*

The painful necessity of the Jay Treaty

The next time someone snidely tells you that republics cannot formulate and keep to a specific foreign policy, be sure to tell the doubter the story of George Washington. For beneath all the surface tumult, the basic realist foreign policy orientation outlined by our first president held in place for more than 100 years, paving the way for America's emergence as a great global power. Almost wholly undetected by today's commentariat—so quick to demean America's past—a long-term US foreign policy was conceived, established, and successfully acted upon by America's Founding Fathers, standing the test of time for the coming century.

This process began with the highly controversial 1794 Jay Treaty, negotiated between the early American republic and Great Britain, the global superpower of the day. It is not too much to say that this seminal event helped send the American rocket into the stratosphere. As tensions built between London and Paris following the advent of the French Revolution, Americans in general were at first broadly inclined to support the French.

The reasons for this were emotional, ideological, and thoroughly understandable. France had been the indispensable ally of the American revolutionary cause, supplying the hard-pressed Continentals with troops, naval support (helping win the decisive Battle of Yorktown), and most of all, the finances to keep the rebellion going through some very dark days. Many Americans, including Francophiles Thomas Jefferson

16

and his right-hand man, James Madison, felt an immense personal debt of gratitude to the country for all that it had done to sustain the American cause.

Beyond this warm personal history, there was also the ideological fact that the French Revolution, bloody and chaotic as it quickly became, was at least founded on the same universalist principles of liberty, equality, and fraternity that had guided the American revolutionaries to their own miraculous victory. It would have taken hearts of stone for the American founders *not* to have felt a genuine affinity with the French for what they were so mightily attempting to accomplish with their own rebellion. In contrast, conservative, monarchist, elitist Britain—so recently America's sworn enemy—served for many such as Jefferson as the glaring counter-example that the new country must avoid degenerating into at all costs.

However, fortunately for the US, Alexander Hamilton—Secretary of the Treasury and the dominant figure in Washington's glittering admin-istration—possessed a head as well as a heart. In many ways, the careers of both the Father of his Country and his headstrong, brilliant protégé amount to a curious throwback to America's earlier colonial days. For they served as bridge figures, linking the country's staid colonial past to its future as a rough-and-tumble republic.

In essence, Washington effectively served as America's last king, with Hamilton playing the role of prime minister, his influence venturing far afield from his theoretically specific purview as treasury secretary. Fascinatingly, their great, joint success in creating and then sustain-ing the viability of the American republic made the need for these two founding giants unnecessary in the future, as it would now be the insti-tutions they had forged and not individual great men that would make the country secure. But to give these nascent national institutions time to organically take root and flower, it was absolutely vital that America hew to a foreign policy that would not endanger its promising experiment in self-government.

Above all, for Alexander Hamilton this meant that the booming young republic had to continue to grow economically. As such, tensions with mighty Britain had to be cooled, to avoid the chaos, tumult, and possibility of outright defeat that another war on North American soil would make very real. With this mandate from Washington, Supreme Court chief justice John Jay was sent to London to bargain with the ministers of George III, resolving the policy issues left unsolved by the Treaty of Paris of 1783, which had formally ended the Revolutionary War.

At first glance, the specific policy provisions of the Jay Treaty seem to largely favor the Court of St. James.[1] The new compact failed to end impressment, the hated British practice of kidnapping American sailors on the high seas, forcibly recruiting them into the Royal Navy. Economically, London was given most-favored-nation trading status for its exports to the US, even as the same economic advantage was not reciprocated for American goods. Jay also failed to win British compensation for southern planters for slaves who had been taken back to Britain and liberated at the end of the war. As Jay was an ardent abolitionist, it is an open question as to whether he pushed this diplomatic point very hard. Nonetheless, the failure riled southerners against the treaty in general.

Yet, for all of its imperfections, the Jay Treaty was an undeniable success for America. England finally consented to leave all US territory, evacuating the frontier forts it still held in northwestern America (today's Michigan, Indiana, and Ohio). Their continued occupation of forts Detroit (Michigan), Niagara (New York), and Maumee (Ohio)—plus the British selling of arms to the various Indian tribes on the frontier—had greatly impeded American immigration into its western territories. In terms of trade, London did throw the Americans a bone, consenting to open the lucrative British West Indies shipping routes to small US ships. American merchants were also compensated for goods confiscated by the British navy on the high seas, where more than 3,000 ships had seen their cargo seized.

But beyond this decidedly mixed record of haggling over the tactical planks of the deal, one great strategic point loomed large, which informed Hamilton's passionate defense of the deeply unpopular treaty. The accord definitively stopped the slide of the two countries toward war, as the weight of these unresolved issues could well have lit the spark that would have plunged the new republic into chaos and calamity. For that overarching reason above all else, Washington's administration decided to back the accord. Simply put, it was undoubtedly in American interests to do so.

The politics of this emotive issue were not easy, to say the least. It took all of Washington's unparalleled prestige and credibility with his countrymen to see the treaty through the Senate, which debated it in secret in June 1795. In the end, the Jay Treaty was ratified by the necessary two-thirds Senate majority, 20-10, without a vote to spare.

However, as the constitutional process moved along, the specific terms of the pact were leaked to a furious public in early July. As the mortified Jay reported, such was the displeasure of the American people with the accord that, by July 4, 1795, he had been burned in effigy in so many towns that he could have traveled the entire length of America by the glow of his own flaming figure.[2] Things got so bad in terms of public opinion that in that same month, pro-French protestors hurled stones at Hamilton while he attended a pro-treaty rally in New York City. Washington described the public reaction to the pact "as that of a mad-dog ... everyone ... seems engaged in running it down."[3]

Given the howl of popular indignation, unsure of what to do—even questioning whether he should sign the accord in the face of the firestorm of condemnation that shook America following the publication of the treaty's details—Washington called on Hamilton, as he had so many times before, for advice. Hamilton, having just returned to his law practice in New York, replied in typical fashion with a masterful fifty-three-page political risk assessment, urging the wavering president to sign the imperfect but vital agreement.

Washington kept his nerve, focusing on the key national interest rationale that he wasn't about to risk the fruits of the revolution on a second war with London. The president also saw that the treaty would prevent a harmful deterioration in trade with Great Britain, on which the United States was entirely economically dependent, as Britain was by far America's largest commercial partner. Once the still wildly popular Washington made up his mind to support the treaty, the overall political debate changed drastically in the Federalists' favor.

Washington duly signed the Jay Treaty on August 18, 1795, with its provisions coming into effect on February 29, 1796. The president made it clear that, regarding America's basic foreign policy trajectory, the United States must—for its own long-term stability—remain neutral in the face of Europe's great revolutionary wars, for the simple reason that not being encumbered by entangling European alliances was the best way to safeguard the country's freedom of maneuver, independence of action, and thus its basic well-being.

However, the furious Jeffersonians were not done with their fervent opposition to Washington's realist foreign policy. Under the leadership of James Madison, Jefferson's brilliant second-in-command, they attempted to block the treaty in the House of Representatives, in terms of not allowing funding for the measures the treaty stipulated. In April 1796, after a full two months of bitter floor debate, a Federalist representative— the great orator Fisher Ames of Massachusetts, "the most eloquent of the Federalists"[4]—strode to the podium. Despite being gravely ill, he gave what is considered to be one of the great speeches in American political history, in passionate defense of the Jay Treaty. It is one of the few examples of oratory on record which actually moved the needle in terms of the political debate.

The House, which had a narrow Jeffersonian majority, finally voted on the measure to allow for funding of the Jay Treaty on April 29, 1796, with the tally resulting in a 49-49 tie. Shockingly, the first Speaker of the House, Frederick Muhlenberg, a dyed-in-the-wool Jeffersonian, voted along with the Federalists to fully fund the treaty.

Once the Speaker's intervention became clear, there were a few more defections, so the final vote in the House for the treaty stood at an achingly thin 51-48. Such were the passions aroused by the Jay Treaty that Muhlenberg's vote obliterated his career; he never held any public office again. In fact, after the vote he was violently stabbed by his brother-in-law, who believed his errant relative was committing high treason. Muhlenberg's extreme case was not the only example of the passions of the day. After the Jay Treaty vote, Washington never spoke to Jefferson or Madison again.

The domestic political consequences of the Jay Treaty controversy were long-lasting, leading directly to the first party system of the United States. The treaty became a core issue dividing the two nascent political parties. Both the Federalists (who supported the Jay Treaty) and the Jeffersonians (who opposed it) became far more organized after the tumultuous days surrounding the treaty's ratification, and then remained so. The Federalists were seen as being broadly pro-British, with the Jeffersonians strongly inclining to a more pro-French foreign policy stance. Never again would the republic operate without two broadly opposed and organized parties endlessly battling to secure political power. The Jay Treaty was that important a domestic political event.

For in the eyes of the Jeffersonians, the Jay Treaty was responsible for the US linking itself to the hated British and betraying old ally France, even as for the Federalists, the treaty saved the emerging nation from a ruinous war with the superpower of the day. These two strong views simply could not be politically reconciled.

Hamilton, characteristically, led the Federalist intellectual charge. Writing as "Camillus" in *The Argus*, he baldly accused the Jeffersonians of wanting to entangle the US in war against the British on the side of the French. He logically argued that the young republic simply could not afford the costs of war with the era's superpower, whatever one's feelings happened to be. What mattered were American national interests, not the emotions of the moment. For Hamilton, competition among sovereign states and power politics were simply realist facts of life, with an interest-based American foreign policy logically springing from them.

However, beyond the politics, in practical policy terms there is little doubt that the treaty proved a success for the young American republic. The Jay Treaty did avert war with Britain, as Hamilton had predicted. Over the next generation, the American economy prospered, due to a boom in trade with London.

Even its arch-foe Thomas Jefferson did not repudiate the agreement when he became president in 1801, a sure sign of its efficacy. The treaty was an unmitigated success, buying America more than fifteen years of peace and ever-increasing commerce with Great Britain in the midst of the French Revolutionary Wars and the rise of Napoleon. As historian Joseph Ellis astutely notes, the Jay Treaty "bet, in effect, on England rather than France as the hegemonic European power of the future, which proved prophetic."[5] Over the longer term, Washington's strategic wager bore fruit for America. As Ellis states, "it linked American security and economic development to the British fleet, which provided a protective shield of incalculable value throughout the nineteenth century."[6]

In the end, Washington and Hamilton's realist insistence on leaving emotions at the door—instead coolly and soberly assessing that basic American national interests were furthered by the US avoiding entangling alliances, even when such a move ran counter to American passions and ideological proclivities—carried the day. With historical hindsight, it is safe to say that the republic itself was the great benefactor. As historian Ron Chernow states, "With the Jay Treaty, Washington had made good on his solemn oath to maintain peace and prosperity during his presidency"[7]—a state of affairs that made possible the steady rise of America, ultimately to the position of the world's greatest global power.

Washington's Farewell Address

But America's Founding Father remained deeply troubled by the very personal attacks that had befallen him as a result of the Jay Treaty controversy, easily the most controversial crisis of his highly successful presidency. Things had gotten so bad that Jeffersonians openly (for the first time) stopped drinking the heretofore customary toast to the president's health after dinner. As his presidency entered its final days, for one last time Washington felt the need to explain himself to the American public. The result was his Farewell Address, a magnificently straightforward defense of his uniquely American realist strategy.

On its surface, the address amounts to an open letter written by Washington to the people of the United States near the end of his second term, before heading into final retirement on his Mount Vernon estate in Virginia. However, the address—originally published in the *American Daily Advertiser* on September 19, 1796—functions as something far more. It gives us a glimpse of the realist credo that steadily guided all of Washington's actions during his momentous presidency. As was so often the case, Washington turned to Hamilton, his long-time intellectual collaborator, to craft the address, even as its major themes remained distinctly his own.

The brilliant Hamilton would play a major role in the address's success. He began work on the speech with a series of notes the president had given him that sounded both petulant and defensive. Hamilton's writing erased this off-putting tone. He wrote a letter that reads as a coolly statesmanlike document, the final valedictory words of a self-assured man speaking for the last time to posterity, after twenty years' service to his country. It was the advice of a "parting friend"[8] on what were the greatest long-term threats to the country to which Washington had given his life.

The address opens with Washington informing his countrymen that he will not run for a third term as president, despite the fact that he almost certainly would have overwhelmingly won re-election again. The president sketches out broad, strategic vistas, imagining America's destination, its grand future as a perennial global great power. To secure the country's long-term political stability—his overriding realist goal—Washington argues that a series of dangers must still be overcome. America's national identity must come to supplant sectional attachments, law and order must be strictly maintained, and something must be done about the evils of political parties, which he warns against and sees—incorrectly, in history's verdict—as a sign of domestic decay.

But beyond all this, Washington stresses that America's boundless western territories—the almost limitless geographical patrimony that ensured its future position as a perennial great power in the world—must be kept free at all costs from foreign encroachments. In other words, while the US must guard its internal cohesion, externally it must also not become a carbon copy of Europe, an area of limited space endlessly fought over by a large number of powers, as no one was able to exercise enduring political dominance over the continent. The US's unique geopolitical gift of sole dominance of North America must be safeguarded at all costs. Everything must be done to secure this unparalleled advantage that luck and providence had bestowed upon the American people.

It is within this broader realist geopolitical context that the president's actions over the Jay Treaty become explicable. For Washington and Hamilton, US foreign policy had to be based, above all else, on practical interests rather than ideological or emotional passions of any sort. As Washington said in the address about the Jay Treaty, in a not-so-subtle dig at Jefferson's emotional Francophilia, "The nation which indulges towards another an habitual hatred, or an habitual fondness, is in some degree a slave."[9]

In the light of his view that neutrality remained the best strategy for America to safeguard its western frontier, suddenly Washington's entire foreign policy becomes crystal clear. He was not for neutrality for neutrality's sake; rather, given the highly favorable specific geopolitical position the US found itself in during the 1790s, such a practical realist policy was simply the best course of action for the young republic. It was because of its geopolitical position, in other words, that as Washington put it, "'Tis our true policy to steer clear of permanent alliances with any portion of the foreign world."[10]

Like any good realist, not only could Washington see the grand strategic picture, he also kept his eyes firmly on the geopolitical prize in day-to-day matters. America could successfully pursue a neutralist foreign policy specifically because it had two moats protecting it from easy foreign encroachments: the Atlantic and Pacific oceans.

The other opposing internal forces that might work against American continental hegemony—Canadians, Mexicans, and the various Plains Indian tribes—were obviously not going to be able to stop the American republic over the long term from dominating the whole of the North American continent. The only other outside forces that could do so were the great European powers. The president was urging the American people to take advantage of their isolated position in the world to avoid permanent attachments and entanglements with foreign powers, especially the great powers of Europe, which he passionately argued had little or nothing to do with these primary American interests.

Given this unique and highly advantageous geopolitical position, all the United States had to do was not mangle its foreign policy too badly, giving major European powers no diplomatic excuse to intervene in far-off America. As such, permanent and entangling alliances with one or another of the European powers was the only foreign policy mistake that really needed to be avoided, as it was the only policy that could conceivably compel a major European power to intervene on the North American continent.

To make such a disastrous outcome far less likely, neutralism in terms of foreign alliances made eminent realist sense. For if the US had no sworn

European enemies, its dominance in North America was almost sure to follow. For Washington, as must remain true for all American realists, loving or hating any specific foreign power—and entering into foreign alliances—should always come a poor second to what really mattered: furthering the specific interests of the American people.

Why Washington's views on alliances and interests must continue to resonate

A foreign policy based on neutrality would safeguard against the only calamity that could possibly derail America's almost unbearably bright and inevitable future as a great power—as master of the North American continent. It is in this realist light that both Washington's highly successful foreign policy and his Farewell Address should be viewed. The Jay Treaty was the practical culmination of this realist strategy affirming America's neutrality vis-à-vis both Great Britain and France by correcting the emotional pro-French tilt that had characterized US foreign policy since the dawn of the republic.

Washington's foreign policy strategy proved so successful that it was not until the founding of the North Atlantic Treaty Organization (NATO) in 1949 that the US dispensed with the first president's advice, entering into a permanent military alliance with most of Western Europe. By then, Washington's impossible dream of America's halcyon future—made so explicit in the Farewell Address—had come to pass, largely as a result of his realist policies.

But that does not mean that we can remotely afford to dispense with Washington's sage realist advice, wrongly viewing it—as today's discredited foreign policy establishment does—as merely the relic of a bygone age. Decision-makers must still look on permanent alliances with great skepticism, while even temporary alliances must be shown to explicitly serve the interests of the American people.

For today's Jeffersonian and Jacksonian schools of thought are united in rightly criticizing the performance of the country's present foreign policy blob, as the center-left Wilsonian establishment has yet to meet an intervention it didn't like. That establishment has been eager to tie America's hands with enduring commitments to countries and regions that are of peripheral interest to the country at best.

Even NATO, the centerpiece of America's permanent alliance structure, should still be judged by the first president's exacting realist standards. NATO expansion should not be some parlor game played by the blob to fill in the geographic blanks on the map *ad infinitum*, ruinously expanding US commitments to countries that take from, rather than add to, the alliance's security. From an American point of view, this is the simple and exclusive yardstick that should be applied to any candidate's accession chances. Is it a security-taker or a security-maker from an American perspective?

Beyond the expansion issue, the further, challenging realist question that George Washington presents us with is, in this new era, whether the alliance as a whole still is fit for purpose, serving primary American interests. Here, rather than repeating the brain-dead catechism that NATO is inherently wonderful, it is instructive to look at the views of Dwight D. Eisenhower, NATO's first military commander.

As Jean Edward Smith's magisterial biography of Ike, *Eisenhower: In War and Peace*, makes clear, the NATO alliance was initially designed primarily as a tool to help Western Europe get back on its own two feet, especially in political terms, and not to be a straitjacket put in place to infantilize the continent for perpetuity. Eisenhower, well aware of the grievous Soviet losses suffered at the hands of the Nazis in World War II, was not overly concerned with a westward Russian invasion into Europe.

Rather, his strategic focus revolved around possible internal communist subversion in France and Italy. NATO was to provide hard-pressed Western European leaders with the limited strategic assurance necessary to overcome their domestic political (communist) enemies. As Smith

27

summarized Ike's views: "The United States was their partner but ... in the end Europe would have to be defended by Europeans."[11]

The point was precisely the opposite of the strategic infantilization that has occurred in practice now for almost four generations. NATO was established to "encourage the eleven European members ... to raise the forces that would be necessary to convince the Soviets that Europe was prepared to defend itself."[12] Ike put it best when he said America "cannot be a modern Rome guarding the far frontiers of empire with our legions."[13]

Almost seventy-five years on, it is surely an open question, and deserves serious strategic debate at the highest levels of the American government, as to whether NATO remains fit for purpose in our new era. For it clearly looks like—long after NATO succeeded in terms of Eisenhower's original, limited, strategic aims—that it has instead morphed into something else, enabling many in Europe's elite to become strategic free-riders.

After personally listening to twenty years' worth of lame excuses as to why Europe could not spend a reasonable 2 percent of its GDP on defense, I said in frustration to a senior German defense official that my high school football team could take your army. For European allied defense spending simply doesn't pass the laugh test. In 2022, of the significant powers only the US, Poland, and the UK met the 2 percent threshold. In contrast, France was close at 1.9 percent, while Germany (1.4 percent), Italy (1.5 percent), and Spain (1 percent) didn't even try.

It is fanciful to continue to expect Europe—all historical facts over decades to the contrary—to suddenly stop being lotus-eaters, and take up a fair defense burden due to the Ukraine war, or anything else. Instead, all empirical facts point toward a darker truth. Europe and its elites deeply enjoy the benefits of free-riding off the American taxpayer and don't really want that situation to change, as it allows them to fund their ridiculously cushy and inefficient economies, leaving defense burdens to their American allies. Obviously, this state of affairs is highly deleterious to the US and its people, and must come to an immediate end.

Secondly, and even more importantly, NATO's European members do not get much bang for their limited buck, inefficiently duplicating what spending they do manage. Not every European country needs a frigate. Solving this problem ought not to be beyond the wit of man, yet the continent's defense deficiencies have persisted for generations. NATO's European members have more than three times as many people as Russia does and more than ten times Russia's GDP. Even given their puny outlays, they currently collectively spend three to four times what Moscow spends on defense every year.

Given these power realities, if properly organized and led—as French president Emmanuel Macron has made clear—there is no doubt that Europe can conventionally defend itself against Russia on its own, with America keeping its security guarantee in place only for the direst emergencies, serving as the alliance's offshore balancer of last resort. A radical rethink of NATO moving ahead, as the US rightly focuses on the increasingly pivotal Indo-Pacific, is now not a luxury, but a necessity. In other words, George Washington's laser-like focus on American interests determining alliance outcomes must once again become the centerpiece of American strategic thinking, certainly for the emerging Jeffersonian-Jacksonian alliance in conservative circles.

As for constructing new permanent alliances today, both Jeffersonians and Jacksonians can unite around casting a leery eye at such an outcome, which has become almost the mindless, reflexive position of the Washington foreign policy blob whatever the circumstance. Rather than shackling ourselves to other countries in perpetuity, Washington made it clear in his Farewell Address that temporary alliances better serve America's needs, as long as they advance primary and specific US interests.

This is far different from writing other countries a blank check to come to their aid forever, which is only a recipe for what has domestically come to pass over the past generation: endless ruinous wars; eye-watering fiscal deficits; the growth of a huge and largely unaccountable national security state; civil liberties being under threat. The American people's domestic needs have too often played second fiddle to obviously tertiary foreign commitments made by a dangerously out-of-touch center-left foreign policy elite.

Washington sent us on a different path with his marvelously calibrated views about foreign alliances, a form of American realism that well served the republic. Above all, if we are to recover from the ruinous excesses of the past generation, it is time to get back to his focus on the people of this country, and not some other.

~ 2 ~

JOHN QUINCY ADAMS
AVOIDS SEA MONSTERS

"No more stupid wars"

Growing up in the long Adams shadow

Louisa Catherine Johnson Adams, John Quincy Adams's long-suffering, if loving, wife of more than fifty years, knew her husband best, shrewdly describing him as "exasperating, tendentious, self-absorbed and yet, in the end, magnificent."[1] But, for all his towering CV and his tremendous complexity, there is a simple key to making sense of the man. Above all else, John Quincy Adams was the child of John Adams.

John Quincy Adams was born the eldest son of John and Abigail Adams, on July 11, 1767. Rarely have a father and a son been so alike in both temperament and historical outcome. Joseph Ellis is surely right in saying of the son that he was "easy to admire but difficult to like, much less love."[2] Much like his father, John Quincy was cold, arrogant, gifted, hard-working, stubborn, supremely intellectual, emotionally stunted, intensely patriotic, and aloof, if passionate about his beliefs beneath it all.

Both of his equally formidable parents chained him from birth to an absolutely impossible standard of perfection. From childhood on, it was made entirely clear to the gifted boy by his talented family that him becoming anything less than President of the United States would be seen as a great disappointment. They raised him to excel, not to be happy.

And excel he did. Of all our American chief executives, he is perhaps the one with the most glittering pre-presidential résumé, speaking fully nine languages. The son spent much of his youth in the courts of Europe, where his father was serving as a diplomat for the American revolutionary cause. During his lifetime, John Quincy Adams served as a Harvard professor, a successful lawyer, minister to a number of European capitals (including being picked by Washington to serve as ambassador to the Netherlands at the incredibly young age of twenty-seven), as well as being chosen by President Madison to help negotiate the Treaty of Ghent in 1814, which ended the War of 1812 with the British on reasonably favorable terms.

In addition, Adams was a congressman, a senator, and arguably America's greatest Secretary of State of all time. Eerily like his father, the only real blot on a lifetime of breathtaking success was a middling-to-poor record as president, from 1825 to 1829.

But it is his triumphal period as James Monroe's highly effective Secretary of State (1817–25) that concerns us most here. John Quincy Adams took Washington's realist foreign policy—predicated on a policy of neutrality abroad and unity at home—and fashioned it into a grand strategy that was to characterize US doctrine for the best part of the rest of the nineteenth century. Just as Hamilton had foretold, this left America the dominant great power on the North American continent. For it was Adams who updated Washington's realist beginnings for the country, making them fit for purpose for several post-revolutionary generations.

Taking advantage of Spain

Forging a strong working partnership with President James Monroe, John Quincy Adams settled into his starring role as Secretary of State. Here Adams faced three changes to the global power structure that he had to accept and then master to further America's interests. First, after the field of Waterloo, Europe was turning inward, above all else desiring peace and stability after the tumult of the Napoleonic age.

Second, Spain, devastated by the Peninsular War of 1807–14, was a declining power, unable and unwilling to defend its far-flung colonies in the Western Hemisphere. As Spain's power shrank, revolutions stirred throughout the whole of its restive Latin American empire.

Third, the British navy was the supreme military force of the age, able to deter any European continental rival from intruding in the Western Hemisphere if London so chose.

Adams was to creatively take these basic facts of life of his time, and use them to craft the Monroe Doctrine, to the great strategic advantage of his country.

While, in 1810–13, Spain was convulsed with internal civil war as it sought to throw off the yoke of Napoleon, the US annexed and invaded West Florida (today's Florida Panhandle). At the same time, the Spanish presence in East Florida dwindled merely to control of its coastal cities and the capital, San Agustín. In practice, the interior of East Florida was dominated by the Seminole Indian nation.

Following Seminole raids along the Georgia border, General Andrew Jackson was sent by Monroe to quell the conflict. Instead, greatly exceeding his orders, the headstrong Jackson precipitated the First Seminole War of 1817–18, unilaterally seizing the lion's share of East Florida. Rather than chastising the headstrong general and withdrawing, as a faction of Monroe's cabinet demanded, Adams saw that the outcome of the war left the United States in a highly favorable diplomatic position.

In opportunistic fashion, Adams used the leverage Jackson had created to prey upon Spanish weakness with the signing of the Adams–Onis Treaty of February 1819. The accord provided for the US acquisition of Florida, while also defining the boundary between a post-Louisiana Purchase America and New Spain in the southwest, settling this ongoing border dispute. Florida had become a running sore for Spain, which had neither the resources to send settlers to stabilize the territory nor the wherewithal to militarily garrison the colony to protect it.

Instead, Madrid ceded Florida to Washington, in return receiving favorable terms in the settlement of the border dispute along the

Sabine River in Spanish Texas. Washington, while not paying Spain for the cession, also agreed to settle US residents' outstanding legal claims against the local Spanish government—brought about by its failure to restrain the Seminole Indian nation in Florida from attacking American citizens along the Georgia border—for up to $5 million.

However, Spain dragged its feet in ratifying the agreement for two years, hoping to use it as leverage to keep the United States from giving diplomatic or even military support to the revolutions brewing in its South American colonies. The treaty was finally proclaimed in February 1821, twenty-four months after it had initially been signed. Adams had secured a primary interest of the young republic, allowing for its continuing expansion across the whole of North America.

Adams's pivotal Fourth of July speech

In 1821, following this diplomatic triumph, the Secretary of State was invited to give a speech in the House of Representatives celebrating the anniversary of his father's crowning glory, the Declaration of Independence. As is true for American realists throughout time, John Quincy Adams was a firm believer in the country's exceptionalism, seeing the republic as destined to be a shining example of democracy and liberty for the rest of the world. Writing to Charles Ingersoll in June 1823, Adams grandly stated, "The influence of our example has unsettled all the aristocratic governments of Europe. It will overthrow them all without a single exception."[3]

However, and critically, realists do not feel the need to actively and militarily export the American Revolution to others; it is more than enough for it to serve as an example and inspiration for the rest of the world. On July 4, 1821, speaking in the Capitol to the Congress and the citizens of Washington, Adams carefully crafted a realist speech that celebrated the unique American founding, while at the same time attacking the legitimacy of both autocracy and colonialism.

Beyond these historical generalities, the Secretary of State was speaking about the quite specific policy realities that he was confronting at the time of his address. In 1810, after Napoleon invaded Spain, imposing his older brother Joseph on the country as the new king, revolutions spread like wildfire throughout Spain's Latin American colonies. As had been true with the French Revolution a generation before, these Latin American uprisings were immensely popular in the US. Many Americans desired to immediately and formally recognize the nascent New World governments as independent states—kindred republican spirits—and to help them in any way America could.

In fact, in 1818, as the Spanish Empire was breaking up, Adams's sometime ally, sometime rival, the political giant Henry Clay, declared in decidedly neoconservative tones that the US should come to the direct aid of Latin America in its fight for independence. This policy suggestion greatly alarmed Adams, who realized that his Florida treaty would be doomed if the US directly supported rebels in Latin America, be they democratic or not.

For though Adams was firmly against colonialism and in general favor of Latin American independence over time, he was far from convinced these new states would effortlessly or even easily become democracies (history would prove him right). In any event, the internal composition of these new countries mattered far less to the Secretary of State than did the pursuit of specific American interests.

No, Clay's siren song of intervention in Latin America had to be refuted. "By overcommitting itself to foreign wars," writes Charles N. Edel, "Adams argued that the country would pervert its mission of promoting liberty. How could a country promote political freedom, Adams wondered, if it was doing so through the barrel of a gun? How would the republic continue extending its domain westward if it was depleting its energy abroad? The country could best continue in its self-appointed mission by restraining itself."[4]

Adams, then having just successfully completed negotiations with Spain over the cession of Florida to the United States, believed it was in America's national interests to hold back. Doubting whether Spain's Latin American colonies would peacefully evolve into liberal democracies once their freedom had been won, the Secretary of State kept his eyes on the prize of Florida. Adams, in line with general realist thinking, thought societies historically evolved organically and that what was appropriate in terms of the political organization for one country was not necessarily immediately applicable to another.

He cautioned against those zealots who "think it is as easy for a nation to change its government, as for a man to change his coat."[5] As such, American political beliefs must not be imposed on other countries whose specific history might be very different from the American experience. The US simply couldn't continue expanding its dominion westward throughout North America (the country's primary national interest) while it frittered away its energy abroad, cheerleading (or even helping) Spain's former Latin American possessions, in the vain hope that over time they would somehow morph into replicas of the American republic despite their entirely different history up until then.

At the same time, Adams worried that the Latin American revolutions could become a pretext for perpetual European involvement in the Western Hemisphere. As the Napoleonic Wars came to an end in 1815, the Prussian, Austrian, and Russian absolute monarchies formed the Holy Alliance to defend autocracy. They hoped to reinstate Spanish Bourbon control over the restive colonies. Having helped negotiate the end of the War of 1812, "Adams thought the country had been fortunate in avoiding territorial losses, and he prioritized avoiding another war with European powers."[6]

But Adams's critique of America pursuing an overly interventionist foreign policy went further. "As a cautionary tale he pointed to the Jeffersonians of the 1790s who had advocated that the United States fight with and for their sister republic France. This was a policy that, if adopted, would have changed the mission of the United States to exporting, rather than solidifying, revolution."[7] This fault line Adams identified persists today, separating the disastrous adventurism of the neoconservatives from the realist restraint that has rightly dominated conservative American thought for most of the country's history. Adams's overall realist foreign policy strategy explains why the Secretary of State was so gravely intent on avoiding war with Spain and its autocratic allies.

It is within this specific historical context that the Fourth of July 1821 speech must be understood. Adams perfectly captured the essence of American realism in saying, "America ... goes not abroad, in search of monsters to destroy. She is the well-wisher to the freedom and independence of all. She is the champion and vindicator only of her own."[8] In his view, the US should remain neutral in the Latin American independence wars, whatever ideological affinities the US may (or may not) have with the fledgling Latin American states.

Focusing instead on specific American national interests, the US should only open formal diplomatic relations with the new Western Hemisphere countries once the treaty with Spain was up and running. Duly, and in line with Adams's realist policy, the United States rather belatedly recognized Latin American states Argentina and Mexico.

By then, Adams had adroitly secured the cession of Florida to the US. As a practical historical sign of Adams's skill, even after Mexico became independent it acquiesced in the terms of the Adams–Onis Treaty. Without blood being spilled, without firing a shot, the Secretary of State had skillfully managed to wrest the state of Florida away from others to the benefit of America, all the while avoiding direct US involvement in the revolutionary wars of Latin America.

American realism at its best:
The Monroe Doctrine

Serving as the intellectual powerhouse of James Monroe's cabinet, Adams convinced the president to promulgate the Monroe Doctrine of 1823, of which he was the primary author. It boldly called for no further European colonization in the Western Hemisphere, even as the US pledged non-interference in European affairs. With the doctrine, Adams was making crystal clear to the rest of the world what primary American interests were, centered in the Western Hemisphere, and what its lesser interests were—the goings-on of the European continent.

Monroe first introduced this key tenet of US foreign policy on December 2, 1823, in his seventh State of the Union letter to Congress. The president baldly asserted that the New World and the Old World were distinctly separate spheres of influence, spelling out that America's core interests, as is almost always the case for great powers, lay geopolit-ically closest to home. As Monroe explained, "We should consider any attempt on their [European powers'] part to extend their system to any portion of this hemisphere as dangerous to our peace and safety."[9] The power politics lying behind the doctrine amounted to Adams's historical wager in favor of America's future, a vision very much in line with that of his father and the rest of the founding revolutionary generation.

First, in the doctrine, Adams reaffirmed Washington's Farewell Address, pledging American neutrality toward European affairs. Second, the hoped-for lack of European meddling in North America would allow the US to continue in its primary geopolitical goal of expanding westward, eventually coming to dominate the continent. Third, this dominance of North America would organically lead to the US over time becoming the sole great power of the Western Hemisphere.

Crucially, much as Hamilton had earlier understood, Adams real-ized that European interference in the hemisphere's affairs was the only possible fly in the ointment, the only strategic jolt that could upend America's seemingly effortless rise to great-power status, as it geographically lay protected from the rest of the world by the two great moats that are the Atlantic and Pacific oceans.

At the time, Adams had the autocratic Holy Alliance precisely in mind as the only repressive political force that, if it chose to intervene in support of Spain's efforts to regain control of its recalcitrant Latin American colonies, could upend America's sunlit future. The Monroe Doctrine was aimed squarely at this repressive alliance, warning it to keep out of the hemisphere's affairs.

Ironically, and painfully clear at the time, America was in no position to even begin to enforce the sweeping claims of the doctrine. Happily for the United States, Britain—the superpower of the day—had interests that singularly lined up with Monroe's bold pronouncements. London feared its vital trade links with the New World would be imperiled if the Holy Alliance or other combinations of European powers further colonized the Americas.

Specifically, London worried that if the newly independent Latin American states became Spanish colonies once again, British access to these markets would be cut off due to Spain's traditional protectionist trade policy. As the Royal Navy was then the preeminent power projection force in the world, America's basic interests articulated in the Monroe Doctrine were to be given strategic substance by the British, who tacitly supported it for their own reasons, for the better part of the rest of the nineteenth century.

But while this was the objective reality, Adams urged Monroe (against the advice of former presidents Jefferson and Madison) not to make America's unspoken strategic alliance with the British more formal. In line with Washington's plea that the US not end up in the pocket of any one European great power through an entangling alliance, Adams convinced Monroe to make the doctrine public, without making a joint diplomatic statement with London, as a clear example of unfettered American sovereignty.

While there were some efforts to overturn the doctrine, such as a move by Napoleon III's France into Mexico (1862–7, as the US was preoccupied by the Civil War) and the failed Spanish efforts to recolonize the Dominican Republic (1861–5), by and large, quite incredibly, its basic precepts held.

The payoff for America was just as John Quincy Adams, keeping faith with the Revolutionary War generation's initial political risk bet, had foreseen. An America free from involvement in endless, destructive European wars and liberated from that continent's interference came to dominate the whole of both the North American continent and the Western Hemisphere, just as they had predicted.

*   *   *

In policy terms, Adams's triumphal period as one of America's greatest secretaries of state was the apogee of his career. As had been the case for the past three presidencies, of Jefferson, Madison, and Monroe, he made his position as the nation's chief diplomat the stepping stone to his successful bid for the presidency in 1824. However, like a Greek tragedy, Adams's victory would prove pyrrhic. The crowded race devolved into a four-way contest between Adams, General Andrew Jackson, Secretary of the Treasury William Crawford, and Speaker of the House Henry Clay.

Given the clutter, no candidate emerged with a majority of the electoral votes. The final tally found Jackson with 99 electors, Adams 84, and Crawford 41. Given this outcome, under the 12th Amendment of the US Constitution, the election was thrown to the House of Representatives, where each state was given a single vote, with the top three candidates being eligible to become president.

With the powerful Speaker of the House, Henry Clay, languishing in fourth place and excluded from the race, Adams managed to win over his critical support, swaying the Congress in his favor. Adams nipped Jackson in the House, winning a majority of thirteen state delegations to seven for Jackson, and four for Crawford. Clay, in turn, was made Secretary of State upon Adams's accession to the presidency, the position that was then viewed as the natural platform to becoming the next president.

However, Jackson, who had also won the plurality of the popular vote, would not go gentle into that good night. Outraged, his many supporters charged that a "Corrupt Bargain" between Adams and Clay had cheated their man out of the White House. With Jackson's adherents dominant in the new Congress, Adams's presidency was effectively emasculated at its birth. The US had never had a Congress before that was under the control of political opponents of the president.[10]

Jackson's men saw to it that almost nothing got done during Adams's hapless term of office. In the rematch of 1828, Jackson handily defeated Adams to claim the White House, decisively winning 178 of 261 electoral votes and an overwhelming 56 percent of the popular vote. Hauntingly, for only the second time up until then, a chief executive was defeated in his run for re-election. The first time, of course, had been the stymied efforts of John Quincy Adams's own father in the face of the popularity of his great friend and rival, Thomas Jefferson.

But John Quincy Adams had inherited one further quality from his famous parents: their fantastic sense of resilience. Rather than retiring following his electoral defeat as was traditionally expected, Adams instead won election to the House of Representatives in 1830, serving with great distinction in the lower house until his death in 1848. While in Congress, increasingly critical of the practice of slavery, Adams heroically sought to get the "Gag Rule" lifted, so that this taboo but central blight on American life could at last be debated in Congress.

Adams also opposed (as did Abraham Lincoln) the extension of slavery into the vast US territories to the West that had been opened to American domination by his groundbreaking statesmanship. Fearing that a civil war over slavery was inevitable, "Old Man Eloquent" hero-ically waged an often-solitary battle against this most wicked of institu-tions. Fittingly collapsing during debate in the Capitol, Adams died at the age of eighty in the Speaker's Room, February 23, 1848. Also fittingly, Lincoln was present at Adams's death, as the torch was symbolically passed to the next American generation.

The promise and the peril of avoiding stupid wars

Following its victory in the Cold War, in the hubris that befell it due to being the sole superpower in the world, America tragically forgot the lessons of restraint preached so effectively by John Quincy Adams. Instead, it fought a series of wars of choice, rather than strategic necessity. From Humanitarian Interventions on the Wilsonian left (in Haiti, Bosnia, Kosovo, and Libya) to nation-building exercises on the neoconservative right (in Iraq and Afghanistan), America frittered away its dominant posi-tion in the world, spilling copious amounts of blood and spending trillions of dollars in treasure for no real strategic gain.

As Anatol Lieven and I pointed out, "What has failed in Iraq has been not just the strategy of the administration of George W. Bush, but a whole way of looking at the world. This consists of the beliefs [shared by most of the US's foreign policy elite] that America is both so powerful and so obviously good that it has the ability to spread democracy throughout the world; that if necessary, this can be achieved through war; that this mission can also be made to advance particular US national interests; and that this combination will naturally be supported by good people all over the world, irrespective of their own political traditions, national allegiances, and national interests."[11]

This ideological lunacy upended the brief unipolar moment, and has proven ruinous to America's overall position in the world. As I wryly noted during the high noon of Humanitarian Interventions, "It suddenly occurred to me that the failed attempts at nation-building in Haiti, Somalia, Bosnia, Kosovo, Afghanistan, and Iraq were all related; in every case they were based on the same philosophically flawed worldview."[12]

The grand disrupter Donald Trump was entirely on the money in saying the United States in general, and the Republican Party in particular, had to "stop fighting stupid wars." To do so, it is well past time for America's feckless and reckless decision-makers to rediscover the enduring wisdom of John Quincy Adams, presently making clear the country's basic interests in the world, and resolving not to fight tragically unnecessary wars. To master our new era, American military power must be husbanded for use exclusively when these overwhelmingly central American national interests are at stake, and for nothing else.

Both Jeffersonians and Jacksonians in the conservative movement can coalesce around a return to this eminently sensible strategic policy. For Jeffersonians, always on the lookout for internal threats to American democracy, this more restrained view of the role of the US military in foreign policy-making allows for a less overweening state, a less secretive government, and more money for the many internal ills of the United States, instead of going abroad in search of monsters to destroy. Seeing that the country is not ruined from within, a key Jeffersonian precept, becomes far easier if the US is not involved in a series of permanent wars engaged in solely for peripheral interests.

For Jacksonians, holding our fire over the little things (Somalia, the Balkans, Libya) allows the United States to focus on the big things, in order to preserve the American community. In our new era, the Indo-Pacific must be the center of our strategic concerns, where most of the world's future economic growth will come from—as well as most of its future political risk, given the brewing superpower competition between the US and China.

We no longer live in a time, as we did from around 1990 until 2020, of easy American dominance. Then, the strategic cost of ruinous peripheral wars could be seemingly lightly borne. Now, we live in a new era of multipolar great-power competition, with a peer superpower competitor in China breathing down America's neck in the Indo-Pacific, the most important strategic region in the world.

The days of being ruinously childish, of either trying to export democracy from the barrel of a gun (the neoconservative dream) or engaging in Humanitarian Interventions precisely because the stakes seem so low (the Wilsonian dream), must definitively come to an end. The story of John Quincy Adams shows us the way back to a more mature, more restrained, and more successful American foreign policy. Best of all, his American realism is fit for purpose in our challenging new era.

FOCUSING ON THE ESSENTIAL

William H. Seward navigates the Trent *Affair*

Compared with today's establishment blob, which tends to do laundry lists rather than actually making foreign policy choices—doing far too much far too badly—a realist US foreign policy must prioritize. Rather than doing everything tepidly, paradoxically it means being far more aggressive (diplomatically, economically, and even militarily) when primary American national interests are at stake, and far less so when they are not.

The unsung career of Abraham Lincoln's Secretary of State, William H. Seward, underlines this vital commandment for remaking American foreign policy along realist lines. Seward's tragedy was always to be on the cusp of greatness. In 1860, a far more well-known national figure than Lincoln, he was the overwhelming favorite to be both the newly minted Republican Party's nominee for the presidency and—given the unbridgeable schisms over slavery in the Democratic Party—the likely next occupant of the White House itself.

But along came the thunderbolt that was Abraham Lincoln, and Seward's assumed place at the center of the Civil War drama was taken, leaving him—as Lincoln's new chief diplomat—as an important but secondary player. In his own lifetime, Seward himself grasped what was to be his historical fate. Years after Lincoln's assassination, when asked by an admirer to show the physical wounds that he carried from that horrendous night in April 1865, Seward heartbreakingly said, "I think I [also] deserved the reward of dying there."[1] Groomed for a star turn, Seward ended up a supporting actor in the American story.

But history's verdict cannot erase the fact that Seward proved to be an able and effective Secretary of State. Above all tasked with stopping foreign great-power recognition of the Confederacy—the very diplomatic success that had won the American revolutionaries their ultimate victory in the War for Independence—Seward managed to walk through a minefield, keeping London and Paris, both sympathetic to the southern cause due to their dependence on cotton, from fatally wounding the Union through overtly supporting the Confederacy with troops and substantial loans.

Attaining this key strategic objective was not foreordained, as Seward was painfully aware that the Palmerston government in England and the France of Napoleon III looked enviously upon a rising United States that was in the process of dominating North America, just as Alexander Hamilton and John Quincy Adams had prophesized. With British Canada to America's north and with the French-controlled Mexican empire of Maximilian to its south, there was a real political risk danger that the US's emerging hegemony on the continent would prove to be fleeting.

Worse yet for Seward, the *Trent* Affair of late 1861 presented the Confederacy with a heaven-sent opportunity to gain the diplomatic recognition from these great European powers that was an absolute necessity if it were to become independent.

Captain Charles Wilkes—a wildly overzealous Union naval officer who may have served as the model for Herman Melville's monomaniacal Captain Ahab of *Moby Dick* fame—entirely without orders boarded a London-based Royal Mail steamer, the RMS *Trent*, and at gunpoint bundled two southern diplomatic envoys who were aboard, James Murray Mason and John Slidell, off the ship and into a waiting Boston prison. The predictable furor that followed in England amounts to the Cuban Missile Crisis of the nineteenth century for the US—the moment of maximum strategic danger.

For in the war fever that followed, it was entirely possible that England and France would be thrust into both conflict with America and, in such heated times, recognition of the Confederacy, which was the one and only strategic outcome that the Lincoln administration had to avoid at any cost. It is to Seward's eternal credit that in the fog of possible war he recognized this, focusing on America's one great interest over myriad less important considerations, and brought the highly dangerous *Trent* Affair to a successful conclusion. Rather than making a laundry list, Seward, a true realist, prioritized the essential, and may well have saved the Union.

A promising start

William Henry Seward was born in New York on May 16, 1801, the son of Samuel Seward, a prosperous upstate landowner. At fifteen he went to Union College in New York, graduating with highest honors in 1820. Educated as a lawyer, Seward passed the New York bar in 1822. Moving to the western part of the state, he set about establishing a prosperous law office and dabbling in politics. In October 1824, he married Frances Adeline Miller, the daughter of the head of Seward's practice. During these early years, Seward became close to Thurlow Weed, one of the first successful political machine bosses in the US, who would come to guide his career as his closest political confidant.

Originally a member of the anti-Jacksonian Whig Party, Seward was elected Governor of New York in 1838, winning a second two-year term in 1840. An anti-slavery man from the start, during his tenure Seward sponsored laws guaranteeing jury trials for fugitive slaves in the state. Elected by the New York legislature to serve in the Senate in 1849, Seward was re-elected to the upper chamber in 1855, joining the new, anti-slave Republican Party. He quickly became recognized as the nation's foremost anti-slavery advocate in the Senate.[2]

In fact, Seward's anti-slavery fervor was entirely shared by his wife, Frances, who became deeply committed to the abolitionist movement. In the 1850s, with Frances as the driving force, the family opened up their western New York home as a safe house for fugitive slaves on the Underground Railroad, on their way to safety in Canada. If this had become known at the time, it would have meant the ruination of Seward's political career.

But this gilded start to Seward's future seemed to be only a foretaste of the feast to come. As the May 1860 Republican convention in Chicago approached, Seward emerged as by far the most likely candidate to secure the party's presidential nomination. Staying home in New York, as was the political tradition at the time, he left his political fortunes in the able hands of Thurlow Weed, who ran the Seward campaign at the convention. However, contrary to received wisdom, Seward was beaten on the third ballot for the nomination by the far less well-known Abraham Lincoln.

There were three basic reasons for Seward's shocking defeat. First, the Republican delegates in Chicago saw Seward as too stridently anti-slavery. While he did not believe that the federal government could mandate emancipation, southerners feared Seward's victory in the election would lead to the forcible ending of slavery.[3] Despite the fact that almost all the delegates were sympathetic to Seward's stance, the panic he aroused in the South meant that any chance a Republican administration would have of keeping the country together would be eradicated with his nomination.

Second, despite his undeniable political talents, Thurlow Weed was seen as a liability by some, as Seward could be painted as a creature of corrupt bossism. Third, it was thought that the Midwest—Lincoln's backyard—would determine the outcome of the 1860 election, which left the New Yorker Seward the odd man out.

Lincoln's allies portrayed him as a consensus second choice to Seward, a moderate in the party whose position on slavery (though ironically the mirror image of Seward's) was less well known, and who might do better in his home state of Illinois, where the election could well be determined. For all these reasons, the unknown Lincoln bested the famous Seward.

Despite what was a gut-wrenching defeat, Seward toiled ably for Lincoln and the Republican ticket in September–October 1860, as he was still the best-known and most popular Republican in the country. Seward focused on campaigning for the Republican ticket in the crucial states of Illinois and Indiana, where he attracted huge crowds wherever he went.

Seward's political loyalty in the 1860 campaign, as well as his role as the leading figure of his party, led to him being rewarded by the new president-elect with the central position as Secretary of State in his new administration, which Seward accepted at the end of 1860.

As Doris Kearns Goodwin points out in her excellent book, *Team of Rivals*, Lincoln had the personal courage to pick a cabinet composed of his political adversaries, but ones of undoubted ability. These included Salmon Chase, the Radical Republican Secretary of the Treasury, as well as Democrat Gideon Welles (Secretary of the Navy). But without doubt, Seward became Lincoln's most-valued "frenemy."

The personal relationship did not start out well. Seeing that Lincoln was including non-Republican stalwarts in his cabinet, Seward wrote to the president-elect that, given the composition of the cabinet, he would have to reconsider and decline Lincoln's offer to become Secretary of State. Lincoln, as he told his private secretary John Nicolay, couldn't "afford to let Seward take the first trick."[4] Shrewdly not answering Seward's note, Lincoln waited until after his March 4, 1861 inauguration to contact his angry would-be Secretary of State. Lincoln asked him to remain, and a by-now calm Seward did. After this first hiccup, they were able to forge a remarkable partnership for the rest of Lincoln's days.

Seward came to deeply admire the man he had once bitterly described as "a little Illinois lawyer."[5] In a June 1861 letter to his wife, Seward said warmly, "The President is the best of us."[6] Goodwin continues: "Seward would become his [Lincoln's] most faithful ally in the cabinet ... Seward's mortification at not having received his party's nomination in 1860 never fully abated, but he no longer felt compelled to belittle Lincoln to ease his pain."[7]

The two men became close personal companions. Lincoln would often go unannounced to Seward's house and relax there before the fire, these two great raconteurs chatting about anything and everything. While Mary Lincoln, who hated most of her husband's companions, was not a friend, Seward grew close to the president's two small sons, Willie and Tad, to whom he bequeathed the priceless present of two cats.

Professionally, this personal regard carried over. Seward was allowed to be at the president's right hand when other cabinet officers were discussing their briefs, while they were never permitted to do so when Seward and Lincoln talked through the administration's foreign policy. Politically, the two men became so inseparable that Seward sat alone with Lincoln and his private secretary John Hay when the 1864 presidential returns came in.

Captain Wilkes as Captain Ahab

It was within this febrile diplomatic environment that the *Trent* Affair exploded onto the scene on November 8, 1861. The USS *San Jacinto*, commanded by the fanatical Captain Charles Wilkes, boarded the British mail carrier RMS *Trent* and at gunpoint removed, as contraband of war, two Confederate diplomatic envoys on their way to Europe: James Murray Mason of Virginia and John Slidell of Louisiana. The diplomats were respectively bound for England and France, where they hoped to convince these European great powers to diplomatically recognize the southern Confederacy as a nation, and to support it financially and militarily in its war for independence.

The Greek philosopher Heraclitus had it right when he noted that character is destiny; it was hardly surprising, given his biography, that Captain Wilkes should find himself at the epicenter of the Civil War's greatest diplomatic peril. Born April 3, 1798, even before the war Wilkes was a well-known naval officer and explorer, and hardly a stranger to controversy. Raised by his ferociously religious aunt, Elizabeth Ann Seton, who became the first American-born woman to be canonized by the Catholic Church, it is an understatement to say that, even for those very different times, Wilkes had a highly pronounced sense of right and wrong and an unshakable belief in his unique ability to judge between the two.

He has been described as a "stubborn, overzealous, impulsive, and sometimes insubordinate officer."[8] Wilkes's character flaws—the very ones which may have inspired the creation of Melville's Captain Ahab— were to get him in a lot of trouble. Far worse, they came to imperil the very chances of success for the Union cause.

After attending Columbia University, Wilkes entered the navy as a midshipman in 1818, being promoted to lieutenant in 1826. Always a man with a decided scientific bent, Wilkes was made a member of the prestigious Columbian Institute for the Promotion of Arts and Sciences in the 1820s, an august body which included ex-presidents John Quincy Adams and Andrew Jackson as members.

As such, in 1838 he was the natural choice to command the US government's global Exploring Expedition a fascinating mission to geographically and scientifically map out the world, with teams of naturalists, botanists, minerologists, taxidermists, and biologists on board Wilkes's small flotilla. The specimens and cultural artifacts brought back by the Wilkes expedition later formed the foundation for the collection that became the Smithsonian Institution.

Sailing the Pacific Ocean, Wilkes explored Samoa, New South Wales in Australia, and most excitingly, sailed into the Great Southern Ocean in December 1839, charting fully 1,500 miles of Antarctica's coastline. While others may have sighted the long-obscured continent ahead of him, Wilkes deserves the glory of being the first explorer to be aware of what he was seeing, truly discovering the Antarctic continent and scientifically beginning to make sense of the world's southernmost landmass. After braving the stormy seas of the Antarctic Ocean for years, traveling 87,000 miles and circumnavigating the globe, Wilkes and his team finally returned to New York in 1842.

However, rather than returning home in triumph, Wilkes made landfall in New York only to be immediately embroiled in controversy, with a court martial trial set in place, accused of cruel, erratic, and imperious leadership during the voyage. He was criticized for losing one of his ships, for habitual mistreatment of his officers, and for excessive punishment of his men. While acquitted of all but one count brought against him in the court martial (illegal punishment of his men), Wilkes's career was sidelined, with his chief preoccupation between 1844 and the outbreak of the Civil War being writing up a voluminous report of his expedition for the navy.

While promoted to commander in 1843 and captain in 1855, the ambitious Wilkes was no longer viewed as a leading figure in the navy. Typical was the view of George Harrington, a senior Treasury official, who warned Seward about Wilkes. "He will give us trouble. He has a superabundance of self-esteem and a deficiency of judgement. When he commanded his great exploring mission, he court-martialed nearly all his officers; he alone was right, everybody else was wrong."[9]

With the outbreak of the Civil War, having been assigned command of the *San Jacinto*, Wilkes saw his chance at redemption. Running the Union blockade from Charleston, the Confederate envoys Mason and Slidell made their way to Havana, where Wilkes became aware they were waiting to board the mail steamer *Trent* for transport to Europe.

On November 8, Wilkes, desperate for the glory that he felt had been stolen from him over his earlier polar expedition, shot first and asked questions later. Waiting to surprise the *Trent* in the Bahamas channel, 250 miles east of Havana, Wilkes had the *San Jacinto* fire two shots over the *Trent*'s bow to get it to stop. He then sent a Union boarding party to the ship, which seized Mason and Slidell before permitting the *Trent* to head on its way. The diplomats were imprisoned at Fort Warren in Boston Harbor following their capture.

The North, desperate for any sort of good news in the war following its defeat at the First Battle of Manassas in July 1861, initially hailed Wilkes's actions as some sort of heroic victory. Northern public opinion celebrated his high-handed actions, rallying against Britain, even with the catastrophic and genuine risk of war looming. On November 26, a banquet was given to honor Wilkes in Boston, and on December 2, Congress unanimously passed a resolution, applauding Wilkes "for his brave, adroit and patriotic conduct in the arrest and detention of the traitors."[10] Meanwhile, a storm was brewing in London over Wilkes's folly, one which carried with it the potential for ruination of the Union.

"One war at a time": Seward salvages victory from the jaws of defeat

William Seward came to his position as the nation's top diplomat with an admirably clear vision of what America's primary interests were in terms of foreign affairs. First, his job was to at all costs prevent European great power recognition of the Confederacy as an independent country. Paradoxically, this had been the American revolutionaries' signal success. After the surprise Continental victory at the Battle of Saratoga in 1777, France and Spain came to recognize the colonies as an independent country, supplying them with critical financial loans and troops to buttress their cause. This proved to be the decisive factor in America winning its independence. Given the country's own history, Seward knew only too well that if the Confederacy was denied this diplomatic breakthrough, the Union's triumph was only a matter of time.

Second, and a corollary to this first point, war with Europe over any other extraneous matters had to be avoided at all costs, as fighting over more peripheral interests would only gift the Confederacy with its independence. Third, while accepting the Union was presently stuck playing very weak cards, Seward had to try to prevent European expansion into the Western Hemisphere as much as possible—in line with the Monroe Doctrine—while the Union focused on its overriding goal of putting down the Confederate rebellion. Luckily for the Union, Seward never deviated from his all-consuming fixation on these primary US interests, never letting other, lesser matters get in the way of his steadfast focus.

Several major factors cut both ways for Seward's agenda. While it was surely true that Britain was interdependent with the Confederacy in the textile trade (the South supplied an overwhelming 80 percent of the cotton for Britain's important textile industry), the North importantly supplied Britain with 40 percent of its foodstuffs. Further, Britain feared an American attack on its isolated Canadian territory. While the prime minister, Lord Palmerston, was an avid opponent of the slave trade, he also believed that a divided United States would strengthen British economic and military power in North America.

As a result of these conflicting imperatives, it is little wonder that, with the outbreak of the Civil War, the British government of Lord Palmerston chose to split the difference, satisfying neither North nor South. Britain announced it would treat both sides as belligerents, allowing it to trade with both North and South. France quickly followed suit. This European policy of neutrality over the American Civil War allowed Confederate ships to obtain fuel, supplies, and repairs in neutral ports, but not be given military equipment or arms.

Fatally, for the Confederacy, neither London nor Paris was prepared to recognize southern independence, which would have allowed the economically hard-pressed South to borrow from foreign lenders. Nor did the mighty British navy challenge the highly effective Union blockade of southern ports, which was slowly strangling the Confederacy.

Seward almost immediately recognized that the *Trent* Affair was endangering the Union's very favorable diplomatic status quo. Predictably, in London, the controversy caused a tsunami, being seen as a brazen violation of neutral rights and an insult to the world's greatest power. First learning of events on November 27, Lord Palmerston began an emergency cabinet meeting by throwing his hat on the table, saying, "I don't know whether you are going to stand this, but I'll be damned if I do."[11] The British demanded the release of the Confederate prisoners into their custody, a formal apology from the American government, and stipulated that the Lincoln administration had just seven days to reply, a message which reached Seward's ears by mid-December 1861.

The Palmerston government moved to quickly back up its strong diplomatic stance with actions. During December 1861, it sent an additional 11,000 troops to bolster Britain's strategic position in Canada. It also banned exports of war materials from its empire to the US, including the crucial export of saltpeter from India, which was the Union's only source of gunpowder. France, while making clear it would remain neutral in any war that broke out between Britain and the US, also urged the immediate release of the Confederate envoys.

Seward, responding to the great realist precept that you should never do what your enemy wants you to do, moved decisively to eradicate the danger of war, even ahead of the usually sagacious Lincoln. The Secretary of State knew he had to diplomatically undo the Gordian knot of admitting fault—as enraged northern public opinion would never have allowed the administration to do so—while at the same time the southern envoys would have to be released if war with Britain, the one thing that couldn't happen, was to be avoided.

Fortunately for Seward, Wilkes not only had been headstrong, he had also acted outside the code of maritime law. This made his actions infinitely easier to disavow. Rather than bringing the *Trent* itself into port to have a court rule on his decision to remove the envoys, as was clearly required by international law, Wilkes had merely waylaid Mason and Slidell, and then allowed the ship to continue on its way to London. This legal loophole provided Seward with an ingenious way out of the crisis. Wilkes's actions could be countermanded precisely because they did not follow the maritime law that America had traditionally held to be vital.

On December 17, Charles Francis Adams,* the able US ambassador to Britain, received Seward's November 30 dispatch stating that Captain Wilkes had acted alone, without orders from the Lincoln administration, a fact Adams immediately relayed to Palmerston's government. Already, the Lincoln White House was distancing itself from Wilkes.

Prince Albert, Queen Victoria's beloved husband and a major political player in his own right, was now drafted in by the Palmerston government to advise them over the crisis. Rightly feeling that the British cabinet's intended response to Seward was too bellicose, the prince (tragically, soon to die in December) reminded Palmerston and Lord Russell, the British foreign secretary, that Adams had assured the British that Wilkes had acted without official orders from the American government.

Wilkes's arrogant boorishness was an example of an officer acting beyond American foreign policy dictates, not serving them. Prince Albert recommended the milder note that was eventually sent, demanding the release of Mason and Slidell and an apology, but in far more measured language. This lowering of the diplomatic temperature gave Seward the political space he needed to craft an acceptable compromise.

At the same time, Seward cast about for allies to bolster his realist line. Senator Charles Sumner of Massachusetts, the respected chairman of the Senate Foreign Relations Committee and a frequent consultant to the White House on international affairs, made it clear to the Lincoln administration that it would have to release Mason and Slidell. He told

---

* Yes, another Adams. The American representative to the Court of St. James was the son of John Quincy, and the grandson of John.

the president that the strategic consequences of failing to do so would be dire: the mighty British navy could break the Union blockade of the South and instead impose one on the North, and the French could well recognize the Confederacy and move into Mexico (which they actually did) and eventually the rest of Latin America. Obviously, this threat to the Monroe Doctrine had to be avoided at all costs.

The key bureaucratic battle came at an emergency Christmas Day cabinet meeting. Seward led the realist charge for calming the waters. First, he reminded the cabinet that releasing the prisoners was consistent with the traditional American position upholding the rights of neutrals on the open seas. In fact, as Lincoln himself noted, the War of 1812 with Britain had come about precisely because of the thuggish impressment practices of kidnapping American sailors on the high seas, much as had just occurred with Mason and Slidell. As he put it, "We fought Great Britain for insisting ... on the right to do precisely what Captain Wilkes has done."[12]

Seward didn't need to further underline the fact that the *Trent* Affair put the United States in a very uncomfortable intellectual position. The envoys would have to be released, but this could be done in a face-saving manner, as doing so was in accordance with longstanding American foreign policy principles. At the same time, Seward agreed with the more hawkish Lincoln that there would be no formal American apology.

Lincoln wrongheadedly clung to the hope at the decisive Christmas cabinet meeting that the US could offer international arbitration for what had happened, rather than abject diplomatic surrender. However, Seward's arguments carried the day and the president admitted that he had no cabinet support for prolonging the crisis. On December 26, Seward's proposal to release the envoys was accepted without dissent.

Adroitly, Seward wrote that the United States would let the envoys go but would not apologize for the *Trent* Affair, which provided the cornered Lincoln government with enough political cover to avoid further serious embarrassment. Seward's reply to the Palmerston government distanced America from Wilkes's actions, making it clear again the overzealous captain had acted on his own. At the same time, the Secretary announced the release of Mason and Slidell in virtuous terms, saying the US would "do to the British nation just what we have always insisted all nations ought to do to us [as neutrals]."[13]

News of the release was published in the US on December 29, with American public opinion being generally positive that avoiding war with Britain was worth the climbdown. By January 3, 1862, Mason and Slidell were once again on their way to Europe. The British accepted that the release of the envoys, though with no formal apology, was a diplomatic conclusion both sides could live with. Seward had salvaged the essential.

There would be no disastrous war with Britain and, as such, there would be no Confederate victory in the Civil War. Lincoln, of course, put it best, when summing up the overriding realist precept for serving primary interests above all else that his administration had come to use over the crisis: "One war at a time."[14] The most serious crisis between the US and Britain during the Civil War had been averted. Explaining the US approach to the *Trent* Affair, the Council on Foreign Relations' Margaret Gach sums it up well: "Often the conflicts you don't engage in can be just as important as the ones you do."[15]

Due to Seward mastering the essential, the tenuous agreement that ended the *Trent* Affair held. British honor had been satisfied over the matter. The Lincoln administration had successfully de-escalated from a potentially ruinous war with the world's premier superpower. The US had defended the Monroe Doctrine, even from the position of strategic weakness into which the Civil War had thrown America. The Confederacy, of course, was the big loser in the crisis, as it had failed to benefit from the sparking of a US-British war that might have led to the Holy Grail: London's recognition of the Confederacy, its only real strategic chance at victory.

By November 1862, with the coming of Lincoln's Emancipation Proclamation (which came into force January 1, 1863), America's image in London had improved to the point that the British cabinet decided to definitively state it would not recognize the Confederacy. Seward had predicted this advantageous diplomatic outcome: emancipation made the abolition-friendly foreign great powers far less likely to interfere in the American conflict.

France followed Britain in saying it also would not recognize the South, unless London changed its mind. Mason and Slidell's mission had ended in abject failure. By 1863, the British position had dramatically changed to the point that London was tacitly supporting the Union. When Seward pressed Palmerston not to let nearly built Confederate ships leave British ports (where they had been contracted), the British government agreed, seizing them in October of that year. It is not too much to say that, in the *Trent* Affair, Seward had helped Lincoln to save the Union.

* * *

Of course, as was true for his immortal frenemy, triumph and tragedy were to follow Seward to the end of his days. On April 15, 1865, even as Lincoln was being gunned down at Ford's Theatre in Washington, John Wilkes Booth sent his minions to also kill Seward and Andrew Johnson, the new vice president. The hulking Lewis Powell gained entry to Seward's house, where the Secretary of State had been convalescing from a painful carriage injury. Claiming he was delivering medicine, Powell tried to force his way up the stairs, attempting to shoot Seward's son Frederick and violently beating him with the gun butt after it misfired. Powell barged into Seward's sick room, where his daughter Fanny was attending him. Powell manically stabbed Seward in the face and the cheek five times.

Private George F. Robinson, assigned to guard the Secretary, gallantly jumped on the physically formidable Powell, forcing him back from the bed and undoubtedly saving Seward's life. Captured the next day at the boarding house of Mary Surratt, Powell was to be hanged with several of the other conspirators on July 7, 1865. But the tragedy had a final cost for Seward. His beloved wife, Frances, died in June, never recovering from the shock of the assassination attempt upon her husband nor the death of the martyred president.

Seward's last years could not rival his gilded partnership with Lincoln, quite possibly the greatest president the country has ever produced. Unlike the great man, the new chief executive—the quarrelsome and out-of-his-depth Andrew Johnson—never sought out Seward's advice. However, Seward was to have one last shining moment. As was true with earlier realists such as Alexander Hamilton and John Quincy Adams, he was an ardent proponent of the United States coming to dominate the whole of North America. To this end, he audaciously bought Alaska from the Russian Empire in 1867, continuing the process by which America came to control the vastness and riches of the continent.

Leaving office as Johnson finished his term in 1868, Seward set out on a round-the-world tour during his retirement, before dying October 10, 1872. It is hard to disagree with the verdict of historian Ernest N. Paolino that, in the nineteenth century, Seward was "the one outstanding Secretary of State after John Quincy Adams."[16] The specific policy reason for this high praise is made clear by Seward biographer Walter Stahr. Seward "skillfully managed the nation's foreign affairs, avoiding the foreign intervention that would have ensured that the Confederacy would become a separate nation."[17] In other words, Seward had mastered the essential.

Seeing the vital

The Seward yardstick for US foreign policy—that American action (or equally importantly, inaction) depends entirely on whether primary US national interests are in play—is in vital need of rediscovery today. In the

Secretary of State's case, avoiding a ruinous war with superpower Great Britain was his primary concern, as this was literally the only way that the Union might actually lose the American Civil War, which was obviously the single most important American interest imaginable.

Likewise, today, the benefits of not acting should be considered far more often, especially given the inbuilt tendency of our feckless foreign policy establishment to reflexively feel that it must always "do something." Too often driven on by the urgent rather than the important, America should instead save its efforts for the few primary interests that matter. For example, in the past decade, despite many in the foreign policy establishment's wishes, the US just about avoided significant involvement in the bloodstained and complex Syrian civil war, which while undoubtedly tragic involved absolutely no primary American interests of any kind.

American decision-makers' higher moral calling is instead to serve as genuine stewards of American blood and treasure.

Ethical realism, and reconstituting a new realist foreign policy for the Republican Party, involves America actually making very difficult but necessary choices based on our country's specific interests, making actual strategic determinations, rather than just agreeing to do everything, as the present foreign policy blob compulsively calls for. That feckless road leads only to imperial overstretch and the definitive decline of the American republic itself. Seward's yardstick must be immediately rediscovered if America's elite is to keep faith with its people in our new world of great power competition.

~ 4 ~

IN BESTING
WOODROW WILSON

*William Borah reminds us that
sovereignty is real and everything*

A very different narrative

It has rightly become commonplace for conservatives to attack the modern-day reality that the left controls the academic world, setting the narrative for the whole of society, whether their story is precisely the truth or not. This is also surely the case in the field of historical scholarship, where the political views of the profession tend to trend somewhat to the left of Trotsky. While the above statement amounts to an exaggeration, there is no questioning the definitive leftward, Wilsonian orientation of the vast majority of historians.

Obviously—and it is maddening that so many of them assume that they have no bias, arrogantly presuming that their views must be universally correct, free from all ideological taint—this pro-Wilsonian orientation colors the stories historians tell. Nowhere is this more the case than in the mythos surrounding their founding father, Woodrow Wilson.

The standard American high school, on cue from the profession's Wilsonian slant, repeats the boilerplate view that Wilson's failure to secure the League of Nations after the carnage of World War I was an unmitigated disaster for both the United States and the world as a whole. In this view, Wilson's glorious and correct vision of a world where war had been outlawed by a form of global governance was killed at birth, the victim of narrow-minded American isolationists, who couldn't see that the antiquated days of caring about their country's sovereignty had given way to a modern world where complex global interdependence made such old-fashioned views more than quaint. Adherence to the Founding Fathers' paramount desire to preserve American sovereignty had become downright counterproductive, even actively dangerous.

Not seeing the prophet's vision clearly, these small-minded national-ists strangled the promising new order at birth, setting the stage for the even-greater horrors to come of World War II, for which they were at least partially responsible. It was only after 1945, so the received Wilsonian wisdom goes, that the United States "got it right," partially ceding its sovereignty by successfully putting into place international institutions (the United Nations, NATO, the World Bank, the IMF, and the various global trading regimes), run by unelected global "experts," who saved the world from a third global cataclysm.

Let me offer you a much-needed realist counter-narrative. For in the story of Senator William Borah's near-miraculous besting of the vainglo-rious Wilson, with all the odds stacked against him, we are reminded that sovereignty, far from being an antiquated, outmoded concept set for the historical scrapheap, remains real and everything.

Presently, Wilsonians around the world—aping their failed prophet—still believe that global institutions such as his discredited League of Nations can somehow replace power struggles between countries with a peaceful system of orderly, technocratic management that brings rule of law to a formerly anarchic world. Today's United Nations, European Commission, International Criminal Court, and World Trade Organization are bureaucratic pillars of the present-day Wilsonian view, all practical facts to the contrary as to their efficacy.

Wilsonians delusionally see these rules-based institutions driving the present world order, which in terms of causation is as if a bird perennially perched atop the back of a rhino thought it was actually driving the big beast, rather than merely taking a ride. For whether they like it or not (and they do not), nationalism (and the sovereignty that sustains it) remains the driving force of international relations, the rhino to the Wilsonians' bird.

The Wilsonians themselves have proven, over and over again, to be dangerously wrongheaded as to how the world actually works. For example, presently near-universal Wilsonian calls in the international commentariat for the rest of the world to get in line to protect the present "rules-based order" over the Ukraine war have been met by an eloquent silence in most of the regional powers. Tellingly, nine of the ten most populous nations in the world, countries like India, Indonesia, Pakistan, Nigeria, Brazil, and Mexico—all with the single exception of the United States—have rejected western Wilsonian calls to support Ukraine. Instead, valuing their sovereignty and their own specific national interests, they have remained neutral over the conflict.

It is Borah, and not Wilson, who understood the future and the timeless truth so often forgotten in today's Wilsonian-dominated academy: sovereignty is real and everything. Be the issue managing America's borders or energy independence, or not outsourcing US decision-making to unelected international technocrats, America must preserve its freedom to act as it chooses to in the world.

The Lion of Idaho

William Borah was born in rural Illinois on June 29, 1865, the seventh of ten children in a large farming family. While the young William was not a particularly good student, he was a born orator, from a young age capable of mesmerizing people with his natural eloquence. Displaying an intellectual restlessness that would characterize him for the whole of his life, as a teenager Borah ran away from home, joining an itinerant Shakespearean company of actors, before his father persuaded him to return. Ultimately, deciding to make the most of his gift of the gab, Borah studied law at the University of Kansas, becoming a lawyer before—like so many of his generation—seeking his fortune out west.

Upon boarding the Union Pacific Railroad in Omaha, uncertain of his destination, Borah—after asking the advice of a gambler aboard the train—decided to settle in Boise, Idaho. Idaho had only become a state in 1890, so the Boise that Borah found was a genuine western boom-town, where rule of law was not yet fully secure. Idaho was a mining state, and Borah made a legal name for himself dealing with the fraught management–labor tensions of the time.

Generally, his view of their embittered ties was that the unions had rights so long as they didn't commit violent acts, making him a rare moderate in an increasingly polarized society. Due to his unique stance, Borah prospered, both in terms of his law practice and by making a name for himself in state politics. In 1895, he married Mary McConnell, the governor's daughter, who remained his wife until his death forty-five years later. They were to have no children.*

Throughout his nearly half century in politics, Borah steadfastly remained a western populist progressive. In 1896, he bolted from the Republican Party to support the firebrand populist William Jennings Bryan for the presidency, before returning to the GOP fold in 1900. In populist fashion, he argued that the people, and not the state legis-lature, should elect senators, though he accepted such an indirectly elected position when the Idaho state legislature sent him to the upper chamber in 1907, a perch he would retain for the next thirty-three years, until his death.

Borah cut quite a figure in Washington, still wearing his western-style ten-gallon hat around this very East Coast town. Borah's striking politics were as distinctive as his dress sense. Outspoken and fearless from the start, he was a strong supporter of Theodore Roosevelt's progress-ive wing of the Republican Party. When Roosevelt's successor, William

---

* Borah was later to have an affair with his close friend, Alice Roosevelt Longworth, the great society beauty and caustic eldest child of Borah's long-time political ally Theodore Roosevelt. Her daughter Paulina was almost certainly Borah's child.

Howard Taft, largely abandoned TR's more populist policies, Borah assumed what would become his favorite role of insurgent, challenging the president of his own party.

During the pivotal 1912 Republican presidential primaries, Borah supported Roosevelt's doomed effort to reclaim the GOP mantle. However, once the party regulars had seen to it that the far less charismatic Taft was gifted the nomination, Borah did not bolt the GOP and join TR's Bull Moose third-party bid for the presidency.

With the Republican Party fatally split between Taft's traditionalists and Roosevelt's progressives, the Democrats and Woodrow Wilson triumphed in the presidential race of 1912. Borah, who personally got on well with and admired the aloof former Princeton professor, leveraged the Wilson years to enact several serious pieces of progressive legislation. In 1913, he helped see to it that the 16th Amendment to the Constitution became law, allowing Congress to levy a national income tax. Borah also, keeping faith with his early Idaho days, helped get the 17th Amendment enacted, which allowed for the direct election of senators by the people.

Given a seat on the prestigious Senate Foreign Relations Committee in 1913, Borah was to occupy it for the next quarter century, becoming one of the country's leading figures on international relations. Shortly after joining the committee, he clashed with Wilson and Secretary of State Bryan over their expansive Latin American policy.

Right away, Borah understood that nationalism was a dominant universal force in the world, including for people from other nations. He worried that there was an ongoing temptation for the US to expand its remit into Latin America, an urge which the completion of the Panama Canal and the chaos of the next-door Mexican Revolution had made almost irresistible. If the US did expand, Borah feared, it meant either the colonization of the locals or incorporating them into the already-existing American political structure—neither of which, he feared, was in the country's interests.

While President Wilson naively assumed Mexicans would not mind American interference in their revolution, Borah, on the contrary, said that if the US meddled, "we must no longer expect to contend with the divided forces of Mexico, but we must expect to contend with the united forces of Mexico."[1] Even early on, Wilson viewed nationalism as an impediment that could (rather easily) be overcome, while Borah more correctly saw it for what it is—a primary driving force of human behavior. They were to have this argument again over the greater stakes of the post-World War I political settlement.

More in line with the president's cautious approach to the world war that had broken out in Europe in 1914, Borah voted with the administration in its initial drive to keep the United States out of the conflict, banning arms shipments to both sides so as not to be drawn into the maelstrom. However, due to Germany's fatal strategic error in initiating unrestricted submarine warfare against American shipping, he reluctantly voted in favor of Wilson's call for a declaration of war in April 1917. However, Borah made it crystal clear that he did so only to defend the country's own specific rights, having no desire to prolong the alliance against Germany with Britain and France beyond the immediate defeat of Berlin and the other Central Powers.

Borah's limited, nationalist call already stood in great contrast to Wilson's universalist claims as to why the war must be fought. Believing that, beyond defeating the menace of Wilhelmine Germany, America ought to have no interest in the British and French empires acquiring more territory and colonies, Borah increasingly pressed Wilson to put forward a statement limiting American war aims. Instead, the increasingly messianic president proffered up the Fourteen Points, one of the greatest examples of strategic overreach in diplomatic history.

The Fourteen Points and the birth of Wilsonianism

Wilson laid out his staggeringly ambitious postwar program on January 8, 1918, during a speech delineating America's war aims and peace terms. But Wilson's fevered vision went much further than this. In quasi-religious terms, it amounted to nothing less than a blueprint for the salvation of the world following the charnel house of World War I. And, given the harrowing context, it is almost impossible from a distance to overstate how popular Wilson's vision initially was to uncounted millions of people throughout the world.

The Fourteen Points called for an end to the many causes put forward as the reasons for the slaughter in the trenches on the Western Front: secret treaties; arms races; protectionism; competing colonial claims; German adventurism. Specifically, the American president called for colonialism to give way to local self-determination around the world, for the French to wrest back from Germany the disputed provinces of Alsace and Lorraine, for Berlin to withdraw from both Russia and Belgium, for the creation of Yugoslavia (even though the birth of this highly artificial "State for the Slavic Peoples" seemed to fly directly in the face of the contradictory president's just-made pledge of self- determination), and for an independent Poland and Turkey. Most importantly, Wilson proposed a new international organization, the League of Nations, whose job would be to (somehow) keep the global peace.

Obviously, such a wildly ambitious program could never come to pass. The cynical premier of France, Georges Clemenceau, put it best. Mocking the self-regarding president, he wryly noted, "Mr. Wilson bores us with his Fourteen Points; why God Almighty has only 10!"[2] In the bitter aftermath of the death of millions, it simply wasn't politically realistic to expect to have a war without victors, as Wilson grandly called for; but nor was there the energy to fully subjugate a defeated Germany, either.

Instead, a dreadful policy paradox emerged, where Berlin was shackled with public humiliation—being forced to sign the Treaty of Versailles, which included a "war guilt" clause—and onerous economic reparations (supposedly covering the damage to civilian property caused by the war), while at the same time it was not fully brought to heel. In policy terms, the Treaty of Versailles fell between two stools: it punished and humiliated Germany without subjugating it. This was the worst of both worlds, becoming a major factor in the rise of the evil of Adolf Hitler.

To put it mildly, the reality of the treaty was not remotely what Woodrow Wilson had so grandly advertised to peace-starved millions. Totally misreading the room, and the desire of both France and (to a lesser extent) Britain to punish Germany and take advantage of their victory in the war, Wilson forgot that human beings, and not angels, make foreign policy. A dangerous, utopian misreading of human nature has bedeviled the foreign policy school of thought that bears his name ever since.

Disappointing as the Treaty of Versailles was (even to Wilson), the president thought he could make good on its shortcomings if his precious league was established. Wilson believed that, over time, an international organization designed to keep the global peace would somehow outlast the glaring contradiction between what he had promised the world and what the Paris accord had delivered.

Tellingly, even before the fight in America over the treaty's ratification had begun, Wilson made a criminally stupid political mistake. Despite the Republican victory in the midterm elections of November 1918, leaving them with a slim majority in the Senate of 49-47, the president arrogantly declined to bring a single representative of the opposition party along with him to Paris, though he attended the peace talks in person.

Rather than having the powerful wind of bipartisanship at his back, due to his own lack of emotional intelligence, the aloof Wilson set in motion events that made Versailles seem to be a Democratic Party treaty, rather than the considered work of American statesmen of all political hues. This was an entirely avoidable error and made it far easier for Republicans to unite, coalescing against Wilson's partisan dream.

Borah at war with Wilsonianism

As we shall soon see, the president's grandiose and disruptive new vision for American foreign policy attracted myriad enemies for myriad reasons. However, Senator Borah was almost unique in his critique of Wilsonianism. Wilson's adoption of the Fourteen Points was intellectually simply an ideological bridge too far for Borah, flying in the face of his fervent belief in an American realist foreign policy.

In a December 1918 speech to the upper chamber, the Idaho senator made it clear that he simply could not in good faith ever support the siren call of either Wilson or Wilsonianism. As he grandiosely put it, Wilson "is in favor of a League of Nations. If the Savior of Mankind would revisit the earth and declare for [the league] … I would be opposed to it. This is my position and it is not a question of personality. It is a question of policy for my government."[3]

Borah was one of the few who opposed the very idea of the league's basis—that permanent collective action was necessary to prevent future wars. Instead, he saw the league as an inherent threat to the foreign policy values of the American founders, particularly around their views of sovereignty and the need to avoid permanent alliances and over-entanglement with foreign powers. Borah saw Wilson's league as a trap that would inevitably involve the United States in all future conflicts in Europe, a direct repudiation of Washington's advice in his Farewell Address and the accumulated wisdom of 125 years of US foreign policy.

Borah's special target was Article X of the league charter, obliging all member states to come to the defense of another member in the event of an attack, if the league's council called for action against an aggressor, through the use of diplomacy, sanctions, or military force.

For Borah, Article X was nothing less than a permanent shackling of American freedom of action, subordinating the US Constitution by giving the League Council the power to commit the United States to war. In Borah's bleak view, American foreign policy would now be the handmaiden of foreign powers with very different national interests from those of the US.

For Borah, this abomination amounted to the ending of American sovereignty, its freedom of action to pursue a foreign policy that suited its specific interests. Inevitably, he thought that signing onto such a pernicious universalist organization would commit the US to fighting in endless wars, without the consent of the American people, superseding Congress's constitutional power to declare war. Borah put his starkly different foreign policy vision plainly: "What we want ... [is] freedom to do as our own people think wise and just."[4]

Though attacked then and now as isolationist, surely this epithet simply does not jibe with Borah's heretofore internationalist foreign policy views.* It is not inherently isolationist to see the need for reserving the right of the American people to decide how to act in foreign affairs on a case-by-case basis, instead of by mechanistically and often disastrously binding the country to specific actions and countries ahead of time.

Borah once said that a man in favor of the League of Nations would also have to be a man who "no longer wants an American Republic, no longer believes in nationalism and no longer desires to see the American flag fly a little higher in the heavens than that of any other nation."[5] In a first-principle manner, Borah was reminding his countrymen that realist internationalism had been the driving force of US foreign policy since the founding of the country, and that ditching its precepts in a headlong rush to embrace Wilsonianism ideationally implied the end of a belief in

---

* It must be remembered that Borah voted for Wilson's declaration of war against Germany in April 1917.

American nationalism. Rather, it would subordinate the republic to an entirely different, and untried, set of ideas.

This sovereign freedom of maneuver, so cherished by statesmen since the American founding, would be a thing of the past if Wilson's league were accepted. John Quincy Adams's Monroe Doctrine, which had ensured America's rise to great power status, would also be obliterated if the US entered into a global collective security organization. As Borah put it, "How shall you keep from meddling in the affairs of Europe or keep Europe from meddling in the affairs of America?"[6]

The simple answer, Borah knew, was that you couldn't stop either eventuality from happening, overturning the whole of the American foreign policy experience up until then and shackling American sovereignty to an unelected international institution whose many members had very different national interests from those of the United States. Borah put it plainly: "All schemes, all plans, however ambitious and fascinating they seem in their proposal, but which would … entangle and impede or shackle her [America's] sovereign will, which would compromise her freedom of action, I unhesitatingly put behind me."[7]

Worse still, the Lion of Idaho could see in the failure of Versailles another European war looming on the horizon. Like a number of other astute observers, such as the economist John Maynard Keynes of Britain, he thought the provisions of the treaty regarding Germany were shocking in their vindictiveness and might well destroy the fledgling Weimar Republic, creating a political risk crisis at the heart of Europe in the medium term. This is exactly what happened.[8] The blank check America was writing for the league, in Borah's view, might soon need to be cashed due to the disastrous Allied terms forced upon a prostrate but vengeful Germany.

For all these fundamental realist reasons, but particularly due to Wilsonianism's assault on the realist notion of upholding sovereignty above all else, Borah was passionately against both the Treaty of Versailles and the League of Nations that it spawned. In fact, despite admiring Wilson personally as a fellow progressive, Borah was so dead set against the ideas lying behind the league that when the president organized a meeting at the White House with the Senate Foreign Relations Committee to discuss the idea and sent him an invitation, Borah politely declined, reasoning that there was nothing he might hear at the dinner that would change his considered opinion, so there was no point in going. The die was cast.

The battle for the league

While the particulars of the fight over the ratification of the Versailles Treaty are complicated, the political outcome came down to one simple power dynamic. Borah and his "irreconcilable" faction—the sixteen senators (fourteen Republicans and two Democrats) who were unalterably opposed to the league—managed to unite with the plurality "reservationist" view, led by Henry Cabot Lodge, the Republican chairman of the Senate Foreign Relations Committee. The preternaturally arrogant Wilson, stiff-necked until the end, disdained meeting the reservationists halfway and accepting any compromises to his creation, thus dooming it to defeat.

This was not a foregone conclusion, given the divisions within GOP ranks and the initial wild global popularity of Wilson's vision. For while the Republicans had won a slim majority in the Senate in the 1918 midterms, they were far from united over their opposition to Versailles and the league. Henry Cabot Lodge, the de facto Republican Senate Majority Leader, a man who distrusted and disliked both Wilson and Borah, became a key player in the ratification drama.

Born in 1850, Lodge was the quintessential Boston Brahmin, serving in the Senate from 1893 until his death in 1924. There was no doubting Lodge's erudition; he received four degrees from Harvard and was a widely published historian in his day. However, if the senator

77

was as learned as the Princeton professor who now found himself as president, he was a match for Wilson also in terms of his arrogance and personal iciness.

A close friend of Theodore Roosevelt, Lodge came to have an all-consuming antipathy for both Wilson and his administration. As he wrote to the ex-president, "I never expected to hate anyone in politics with the hatred I feel toward Wilson."[9] While Lodge joined Borah in supporting Wilson over America's entry into World War I, he attacked the Fourteen Points as unrealistic and the president as hopelessly idealistic.

However, Lodge proved himself politically supple, whereas Wilson was predictably stubborn and self-destructively unyielding. Lodge convinced Borah to keep the Republican Party together,* with the two co-authoring forty-five amendments and four reservations in the Senate Foreign Relations Committee to Wilson's treaty, rather than outright rejecting it. The two focused particularly on Article X of the League of Nations charter, shrewdly suspecting that Wilson was emotionally incapable of accepting any kind of compromise over his life's work.†

As was true of Borah, Lodge feared the United States accepting Article X, which required all signatories to pledge to defend each other's boundaries against aggressors if ordered to do so by the League Council, believing this open-ended commitment would corrode Congress's war-making powers and decisively erode American sovereignty. For both Borah and Lodge, the primacy of American sovereignty was an intellectual circle that Wilson's league simply couldn't square, as US national security interests would then be decisively subordinated to the demands of the league.

While both sides of the debate were internationalists—contrary to the sore-loser, Wilsonian-dominated narrative of the lion's share of today's historians—their visions were diametrically opposed. For Wilson and his

---

* Of course, it had fatally split as recently as the Taft–Roosevelt schism of 1912, which had handed the presidency to Wilson.

† Maddox, pp. 53–7.

followers, internationalism meant collective security and international law. For Lodge and Borah, it meant maximizing America's freedom to act in a perpetually uncertain world. Lodge made it a point in his reservation to Article X to plainly state that alterations to the league's charter must be made, allowing both houses of the US Congress to individually approve US interventions called for by the league in the future, retaining American decision-making preeminence.

In the end, on October 24, 1919, Lodge proposed fourteen reservations (though Borah co-drafted the language) to the Treaty of Versailles, centered around the Irreconcilable–Reservationist concord over the danger of Article X. The Treaty of Versailles was considered by the full Senate in two forms: in a clean bill (as supported by Wilson), and with the reservations (as supported by Lodge and his faction). Only Borah's Irreconcilables made it clear they would not vote for either under any circumstances.

As Lodge's Senate Foreign Relations Committee hearings dragged on in 1919, the political momentum for Wilson's dream began to flag. Still convinced the immense global popularity of his vision could save the day, the overconfident president began a national speaking tour to salvage the league, hoping to use public opinion to force the Senate to approve the Treaty of Versailles without conditions.

Borah, knowing himself to be Wilson's equal in terms of oratorial skills, shadowed Wilson's national tour as a "truth squad," determined to give his opposing view, often outdrawing the crowds of the president as public opinion grew murkier. Finally, in Pueblo, Colorado, on September 25, 1919, the president physically collapsed due to exhaustion, only to have a debilitating (and hidden from the public eye) stroke a week later, which left him partially paralyzed and out of action as the ratification drama came to a climax.

On November 19, 1919, both versions of the treaty came to the Senate floor for the climactic debate. Borah, universally recognized as the premier orator in the Senate, made the case for rejection. Speaking for two hours without using notes, he gave what is generally considered one of the great speeches in the history of the upper chamber, dominating the debate with an address that moved even the emotionally stunted Lodge to tears. He argued that, in accepting the league, "We [would] have forfeited and surrendered, once and for all, the great policy of 'no entangling alliances' upon which the strength of this Republic has been founded for 150 years."[10]

Borah went on to denounce the league as an effort to endlessly enmesh the United States in the complex web of European politics, which had just caused the calamity of World War I. This would remove foreign policy ever further from American public opinion, a reality anathema to the populist Borah. The world was not ready, then or now, to "outsource their vital interests to an international organization."[11]

Borah went on to say that, almost certainly, despite Wilson's fevered claims, the league would not put an end to warfare for all time. Rather— as actually happened in the 1930s—he argued that any nation that perceived the league to be intruding on its war-making prerogative would simply withdraw from the organization. For Borah, as was true for Lodge, Article X of the league's charter was the heart of the matter. He saw it as a scheme to use American military force to defend the present territorial status quo, particularly helping Britain and France secure their far-flung empires against the will of local people everywhere. For Borah, nationalism was a powerful, primal force that could not possibly be controlled by weak yet politically unaccountable international organizations.

As Lodge had cannily predicted, Wilson's arrogance proved to be the undoing of his vision. When urged by his allies to compromise with Lodge over the reservations in order to salvage his dream, Wilson, in otherworldly tones, made it clear that it was the majority leader who was obligated to give way. On November 19, a coalition of Wilson's Democrats (at his insistence) and fifteen Irreconcilables voted down the treaty with the Lodge reservations 39-55, while both the Lodge and Borah wings of the Republican Party joined together to vote it down without reservations, 38-53.

But the Wilsonians were not ready to throw in the towel. Lodge grew increasingly unhappy with the treaty's outright repudiation, and in January 1920, quietly convened a bipartisan group of senators to try to find a compromise acceptable to a majority of the upper house. Upon getting wind of Lodge's treachery, Borah acted decisively, meeting the majority leader behind closed doors and threatening him with the nightmare of a party schism should Lodge go ahead with his clandestine initiative.

Cowed by Borah's threat, Lodge's bipartisan gambit proved to be stillborn. Brought up for a final vote on March 19, 1920, with the original Lodge reservations, the treaty failed once again, though by the much closer margin of 49-35 (with only half the Democrats honoring Wilson's suicidal call to vote the treaty with reservations down), just seven votes short of ratification. As Robert Maddox grudgingly put it, "Borah as much as any man deserves the credit—or the blame—for the League's defeat."[12]

There is little doubt that the fight over the League of Nations was the greatest foreign policy confrontation between Congress and the Executive Branch in the first half of the twentieth century, being the first time in American history the Senate ever rejected a peace treaty proposed by the White House. There is also little doubt that Borah lay at the heart of the struggle. Known as the "Great Opposer," the senator was surely a gadfly, as his opponents charged, being far better at obstructing policy than at creating it.

A great horseman, Borah regularly exercised his mounts in Washington's Rock Creek Park. In the 1920s, President Calvin Coolidge saw Borah riding there, and drolly noted, "it must bother the Senator to be going in the same direction as his horse."[13] The anecdote is funny precisely because it rings true; Borah was an inveterate contrarian. But given the Wilsonian overreach of the time, a brave and principled opposer was precisely what the country needed.

Twilight of the Lion

Unsurprisingly, Borah remained a maverick for the rest of his life. Equally predictably, he often got in his own way. Following Wilson's demise, the senator fought with three Republican presidents (Harding, Coolidge, and Hoover) during the long GOP ascendancy, 1921–33. In an effort to tame him, Coolidge even offered to make Borah his running mate in 1924. Borah, of course, refused. Hoover tried to co-opt the cantankerous rebel as well, offering him the office of Secretary of State in 1928. Once again, in an effort to safeguard his fiercely cherished independence, Borah declined.

With Lodge's death in November 1924, the Lion of Idaho did ascend to a job he had always coveted, becoming chairman of the Senate Foreign Relations Committee. He used his perch to continue advocating for an American foreign policy of restraint, opposing the country's forays into Latin America. However, with FDR's landslide victory in 1932 and with the Republicans a minority in the Senate, Borah lost the important chairmanship, though he remained a member of the committee.

Ever the progressive, Borah liked and admired Roosevelt for his liberalism and his energy, even though he stuck with his increasingly conservative party. Deciding to run for president himself in 1936, he saw a chance to recast the out-of-favor Republican Party along progressive lines. While Borah was the leading vote-getter in the (infrequent) state primaries, the dominant party machine bosses installed Alf Landon, Governor of Kansas, as the GOP's nominee.

Roosevelt won an overwhelming victory, claiming forty-six of forty-eight states. But Idaho was still in lockstep with Borah. In the same year, he easily won a sixth term in the Senate, one of only sixteen Republicans who remained in the upper chamber. Sadly, his last major foray into international relations was his worst. Not seeing that Nazism was an existential threat to the world,* Borah wrongly thought he might be able to help head off world war by meeting directly with Hitler. Blessedly, he was talked out of this looming disaster.

On January 19, 1940, the Lion of Idaho died in his sleep from a cerebral hemorrhage at seventy-four, in his Washington home. William Allen White, a prominent Kansas newspaper editor and an old friend and classmate of Borah's, put it best. He was "a righteous man who was wise and unafraid, who followed his star, never lowered his flag, and never lost his self-respect … an honest man who dedicated his talents to his country's good."[14]

It is hard to think of a better or more fitting epitaph for a man who— far from what the standard, simplistic Wilsonian historical fairy tale regarding the titanic fight over the League of Nations has told us—bested a dangerously wrongheaded president, honorably upholding the primary realist notion that American sovereignty is real and everything.

---

* See the next chapter.

~ 5 ~

FIGHTING WHEN
IT IS NECESSARY

*Franklin Roosevelt saves the
United States from the Nazi peril*

Polio is the making of the man

Even today, my political risk firm intensively studies the life biographies of major world leaders, looking for clues in their personal backgrounds that point to what they are likely to do on the global stage. In the case of the pivotal Franklin Delano Roosevelt, rarely has there been so clear a case of biography explaining not only a man's destiny, but his country's.

It is not too much to say that, until 1921, Roosevelt walked between the raindrops, without much effort leading a particularly gilded life. FDR was born into wealth and opulence at his parents' beautiful estate in Hyde Park, New York, along the Hudson River Valley, on January 30, 1882. The beloved son of doting parents James and (especially) Sara, he spent a happy childhood there, before moving on to graduate from Harvard in 1903. Haphazardly pursuing a career in law, which Franklin spent as little time as possible working at, allowed him to indulge his passion for politics. For Franklin's family were the direct kin of the mighty Theodore Roosevelt, who as president had ushered America into a new coming of age as a great power. It seemed a natural fit that his younger cousin would also enter the political arena.

In 1905, Franklin married his distant cousin Eleanor, Teddy Roosevelt's favorite niece. Their difficult marriage would survive infidelity, tragedy, and cataclysmic political events. For all of this, Eleanor would morph into one of Franklin's most trusted advisers, as she was entirely there for him at the most testing moment of his life.

Ascending the greasy pole of New York state politics (but as a Democrat, perhaps because of Teddy's notoriety as the country's best-known Republican), FDR was elected state senator in 1910, being re-elected in 1912. Following this, in 1913, on the eve of World War I, he became Assistant Secretary of the Navy in the progressive administration of Woodrow Wilson, ably serving in this important post throughout the global conflagration.

In 1920, Roosevelt was nominated by the Democrats as their vice-presidential candidate. While the ticket (headed by Governor James M. Cox of Ohio) lost, FDR made a name for himself across the country, as he successfully barnstormed for his party. Surely the top job itself was soon to come his way. Roosevelt's future seemed destined to be effortlessly brilliant. But politics, like life, rarely proceeds in such a straight line.

In late July 1921, FDR gave a speech to a Boy Scout camp at Bear Mountain, in upstate New York. It is almost certainly here that he contracted infantile paralysis. On August 10, 1921, at his family's summer retreat on Campobello Island in New Brunswick, Canada, Roosevelt awoke with a fever of 102 degrees and severe leg pain. By the evening of the next day, he was paralyzed from the waist down. It is almost impossible to convey the terror polio wrought on Roosevelt. Literally, he went to sleep with a gilded existence, only to awaken crippled for the rest of his life. And yet this horror did not defeat him. Rather, in the odd way of life, it was to prove the making of him.

Up until now, FDR was generally seen by his contemporaries as a charming, able man. But he was also viewed as callow, an intellectual lightweight who glided on the surface of things, leaving the hard work of policy-making (and indeed, living) to other, more substantial men. After Roosevelt's utterly heroic overcoming of polio, literally no one thought of him in these mixed terms again. Surmounting the disease taught him patience, as he discovered the iron will that would always lie just beneath the surface of his fetching smile during the tumultuous years to come. For, during this supreme crisis in his life, FDR found his better self, the man who in 1933 could truthfully say based on his own biography to his shell-shocked countrymen: "We have nothing to fear but fear itself."

The obstacles Roosevelt had to overcome are almost beyond imagining. Due to disuse, FDR's legs atrophied so badly that they bent backward. They had to be put in plaster casts, causing him constant pain. Roosevelt would require fourteen-pound leg braces to walk with crutches for the rest of his life. "Walking" itself became—in typical FDR fashion—more of a magic trick designed to convince the public he was all right than anything else.

Through constant exercise, Roosevelt built up his upper body strength. With the aid of a large man (often one of his sons) next to him, he would rise as his leg braces were straightened. Then, with the help of the man and the crutches, he would approximate movement, balancing himself as he glided forward. It wasn't really walking as we know it, but the effect made it seem as if FDR had somehow overcome polio, and was fit for public service. As ever with Roosevelt, the illusion hid deeper meaning.

While his formidable mother, Sara, urged FDR to retire from public life to Hyde Park where she could look after him, both Eleanor and FDR's chief political confidant—the shrewd, if cantankerous, Louis Howe—encouraged him to stay interested in the public arena. They selflessly devoted themselves to keeping Franklin up to date on the goings-on of American public life.

The test of Roosevelt's continued political viability came on June 26, 1924, when he was asked to speak at the Democratic Party convention at Madison Square Garden in New York. If FDR had stumbled and fallen during his arduous walk across the stage, there is little doubt his political career would have been over. Yet, after practicing for the rigors of the Garden again and again, FDR not only made it to the podium, his nationally broadcast speech was a great success, thrusting him back into the political limelight.

Nine short years later, FDR was president, and it was the Depression-stricken country itself that desperately needed his example of how to deal with bolt-from-the-blue adversity. As has happened so often in American history, the crisis at hand was met by a man of destiny. An immature, untested, shallow, lightweight (if charming) young man had given way to the shrewd, patient, calm, ruthless, unflappable, and iron-willed leader who was to become a political legend. For, in the bitter-sweet way that life can work, Roosevelt could not have become FDR for the nation if he hadn't already surmounted the supreme personal crisis of his life in the 1920s.

Franklin Roosevelt, unlikely realist

As the 1930s proceeded, global depression gave way to the rise of Hitler and Nazism as the great political risk of the age. Here again, Roosevelt found himself ahead of the curve, early on seeing that Germany was a revolutionary power determined to upend the present world order, substituting it with one dominated by the sinister forces of National Socialism. For all his highfalutin Wilsonian rhetoric, at base there is little doubt that FDR was a quintessential realist, trying to update America's organic foreign policy to take on board Nazism's existential threat to primary American national interests.

As anyone who has ever played the game of Risk knows, control of the primary Eurasian world landmass leads to the domination of the planet. Thus, to this day, American grand strategy eerily follows in the footsteps of the prior ordering power, Great Britain. Whereas British foreign policy since the Glorious Revolution could be reduced to the notion that London would always balance with lesser European powers against the greatest power on the European continent, in an effort to avoid its domination, so America adopted this geostrategic precept, applying it to both halves of Eurasia.

As Roosevelt saw early and often, any great power threatening to control either Europe or Asia must be balanced against, by force if necessary, as such dominance of Eurasia would inevitably lead to control over the lesser Western Hemisphere island. The "Roosevelt Rule"—this prevention of the dominance by an outside power of either portion of the Eurasian landmass—was, remains, and ought to be the single geostrategic primary interest of the United States.

In a June 10, 1940 commencement address at the University of Virginia, FDR came as close as he ever would to revealing the rationale lying behind his realist policy. As Conrad Black notes in his shrewd biography of Roosevelt, "He referred to 'those [Americans] who still hold to the now obvious delusion that we can permit the United States to become a lone island ... in a world dominated by the philosophy of force.' Such an island would be like a prison whose inhabitants are 'handcuffed, hungry, and fed through bars ... by the contemptuous, unpitying masters of other continents.'"[1]

Likewise, in his famous radio fireside chat of December 29, 1940, FDR put the case for his foreign policy to the American people in stark geopolitical terms. "If Britain goes down, the Axis powers will control the continents of Europe, Asia, Africa, Australasia, and the high seas—and they will be in a position to bring enormous military and naval resources against this hemisphere."[2]

In other words, America was not wholeheartedly supporting Churchill and the British out of some naive impulse based on charity. The Royal Navy, as it had done since the days of John Quincy Adams, was still de facto protecting the US and the Western Hemisphere from outside European efforts at meddling. If, after British defeat, it fell into the hands of the Nazi high command, it would be an unmitigated strategic disaster for the US. Therefore, the continued existence of an independent Britain (with its navy out of Hitler's prying hands) was obviously a vital US national interest.

So, to prevent America being geo-strategically subsumed by a fascist world order, Washington was prepared to help London by becoming the "Arsenal of Democracy." In a swipe at the contrasting isolationist views of the time, FDR charged, "But we well know that we cannot escape danger, or the fear of danger, by crawling into bed and pulling the covers over our heads."[3]

As the 1930s progressed, Roosevelt understood that Nazi Germany's drive to dominate Europe and (to a lesser extent) Imperial Japan's drive to dominate Asia constituted existential threats to primary American interests. "Roosevelt had recognized from the earliest moments of the Third Reich that Western democracy probably could not coexist with it."[4]

However, he was also painfully aware that his countrymen had yet to reach this conclusion. FDR increasingly understood that fighting for these primary American interests might well prove necessary. Instinctively, "he knew Hitler had to be defeated. No scenario for the elimination of Hitler was ever credible without the full involvement of the United States."[5] The political trick was to convince his skeptical nation that these were interests worth fighting for, and that these were foes worth fighting against.

In the wake of Woodrow Wilson's disastrous efforts at an overly expansive foreign policy, sentiment in America (not for the last time) over-corrected the problem. In the 1930s, Congress passed a series of neutrality acts designed to see to it that at all costs the United States stayed out of the coming European war. FDR's torturous strategy as the decade progressed was to remain credible in his repeated promise to keep America out of the inevitable conflict while at the same time preparing for it.

Fortunately, given this contradictory, almost impossible, political imperative, America had at its helm perhaps the most tactically devious (if strategically principled) statesman the country has ever seen. FDR's modus operandi when confronted with a big policy decision was to talk to as wide a range of experts as possible, seeming to agree with all of them, while never actually committing to any specific course of action they proposed.

Hundreds of people left the White House convinced that the charming chief executive was fully on their side, only to find out later to their dismay he had chosen to do the precise opposite of what they had suggested. Seeing all sides of a problem, playing his cards as close to his vest as he could, Roosevelt used his considerable native charm to distance himself from his advisers, his breezy manner keeping them onside, even as such a way of working gave him the maximum flexibility necessary to act as he saw fit. As Black notes, "Roosevelt was always enigmatic until he had to take a stand, and then he did so with great determination."[6] As was true for later successful presidents, such as Eisenhower, Kennedy, and Reagan, FDR combined a surface amiability with an underlying toughness.

This unique management style suited the times, as Roosevelt tried to belatedly prepare his country for the unpalatable realist fact that when primary national interests are at stake, there are times they must be fought for. Confronted with the greatest foreign policy crisis since the revolution, and despite his Wilsonian sheen, FDR followed a realist course in preparing an unaware America for world war. But it is absolutely clear that Roosevelt understood the nature of the Nazi peril from early on. As he stated as early as December 5, 1938, "What America does or fails to do in the next few years has a far greater bearing and influence on the history of the whole human race for centuries to come than most of us who are here today can ever conceive."[7]

A country with its head in the sand

The political task confronting FDR was formidable. Until 1939, Roosevelt's involvement in foreign affairs had been sporadic at best.

Grappling with the domestic existential crisis of the Great Depression had understandably taken up the lion's share of his time. In that year, the US fielded an army of only 185,000 men, ranking it eighteenth in size in the world. The interwar years had left America essentially disarmed. As a first step forward, FDR wanted the revision of the Neutrality Acts, allowing the sale of US war materiel to Britain and France in the event of war.

Congress had passed three Neutrality Acts between 1935 and 1937. First, they prohibited financial loans to belligerents. Second, they imposed an arms embargo on all parties, regardless of who the victim of the aggression was. Third, even non-military goods could only be purchased by either belligerent for cash, and only if the wherewithal was transported in non-American ships.

As Kissinger would shrewdly note, "As the aggressors bestrode Europe, America abolished the distinction between aggressor and victim by legislating a single set of restrictions for both."[8] Congress was burying its head in the sand, crafting a foreign policy not fit for purpose at a time when Nazi Germany was showing itself to be a revolutionary power, intent on destroying both the whole of the international order and America's favorable place in it.

While an initial attempt to revise the Neutrality Acts passed the House of Representatives, 200-188, it only did so with a crippling amendment that continued the embargo on all arms and ammunition to other countries. Sensing trouble and playing for time, FDR pressed Democrats on the Senate Foreign Relations Committee (who voted 12-11 in favor) to delay consideration of the flawed House bill until the next session of Congress, in June 1940.

In late September 1939, just after the outbreak of the world war in Europe, Roosevelt summoned Congress back into special session, with the express purpose of revising the Neutrality Acts once and for all. Adroitly, FDR managed to reach a bipartisan compromise over a fourth Neutrality Act, which came into force in November 1939. The arms embargo would be repealed, but the sale of any future weapons would be on a strict "cash and carry" basis. There would be no sale of American arms made on credit, no US funding of sales to any of its allies, no American bank loans made to expedite arms sales, and no US transport of the arms.

While it was not an unmitigated triumph, Roosevelt—the master of American politics—was shrewdly willing to settle for the policy movement in his direction that the compromise represented. The fourth Neutrality Act was a marked improvement over the earlier three. A September 1939 Gallup poll found that a decisive 60 percent of Americans favored amending the Neutrality Act, while an overwhelming 84 percent now favored an Allied victory.

FDR knew he had to prepare for the future, even as he waited for the American public to catch up with him. This was no mere tactical gambit; instead, it was the resolution of a man utterly committed to the American experiment in republican government. As Roosevelt told Helen Rogers Reid, wife of the publisher of the *Herald Tribune* and a childhood neighbor and playmate from his early Hyde Park days, "Governments such as ours cannot swing so far so quickly. They can only move in keeping with the thought and will of the great majority of our people. Were it otherwise the very fabric of our democracy—which after all is government by public opinion—would be in danger of disintegration."[9]

At the time, Roosevelt's public arguments about the necessity of amending the Neutrality Act threaded the needle. He maintained that the revision was a step toward preserving peace for the US, while at the same time noting such a step favored Britain and France. The implied realist logic was that arming the Allies to defeat Hitler would allow America the luxury of staying out of the war. At last, the shackles of the previous Neutrality Acts were lifted from Roosevelt, as in October–November 1939, the Senate voted for his new alternative, 63-30, with the House following, 243-181.

Just as aid to the Allies was at last on the table, FDR began America's breakneck efforts to rearm. Within a year, by May 1941, Congress had appropriated $37.3 billion for defense. To put this massive total in perspective, the figure was roughly four times the whole of the federal budget in 1939.[10]

The crucial presidential election of 1940

The key to Roosevelt's political risk success lay in his victory in the 1940 presidential election, when he ran for an unprecedented third term. Since the days of George Washington, tradition had held that chief executives, however popular, stopped—in light of the father of the country's example—after eight years in office. However, given the peril of the times, FDR was prepared to flout 150 years of custom in his effort to prepare America for a war in which its primary interests were at stake.

On the face of it, he needn't have bothered. For the Republican nominee, the forty-eight-year-old Wendell Willkie—exuberant, tousled, vigorous, able, witty, and charming—was eerily in line with Roosevelt's overall foreign policy. Willkie had long been an internationalist Democrat, not joining the Republican Party until March 1939.

Initially a supporter of the New Deal, he had grown alarmed at the considerable new powers that had been placed in Roosevelt's hands as the decade progressed. He believed that the Democratic Party had been steered away from its liberal ideals, as FDR had converted it into a party of centralizers and big government. Due to all this, Willkie saw Roosevelt as a threat to American individual liberties themselves. FDR's determination to run for a third term merely confirmed Willkie's suspicions.

But over foreign affairs, there was little to separate the two candidates. Far from being an isolationist, Willkie had supported Woodrow Wilson's League of Nations and backed unlimited aid being given to the British and the French. Sounding distinctly Rooseveltian, in May 1940

Willkie argued, "England and France constitute our first line of defense against Hitler. If anyone is going to stop Hitler, they are the ones to do it. It must therefore be in our advantage to help them every way we can, short of declaring war."[11] As FDR gravely stated to his cabinet, "I have the general opinion that the Republicans have nominated their strongest possible ticket."[12]

No, for FDR, Willkie was not the problem. While Roosevelt respected and admired Willkie, he was convinced that the machinery of any Republican administration, in the executive and legislative branches, would be in the disastrous hands of the isolationists who made up a major portion of the base of the GOP at the time. Fearing that Willkie, a political novice, would surely lose control of his party over the central coming issue of war and peace, FDR felt that he had no choice but to run for an unprecedented third term. Crucially, Roosevelt also knew that the talented Willkie could have beaten literally every other possible Democratic candidate running for president. To safeguard the future of the country, it literally had to be FDR in 1940.

Indeed, on the eve of the election, the American public were still psychologically unprepared for the coming world war. A June 25 Gallup poll, the day of the stunning Nazi-imposed armistice in France, found that a decisive 64 percent of Americans believed that it was more important to stay out of the conflict than to assist a hard-pressed Britain.[13] Even the Gallup poll of October 20, less than a month before the election, found the country split down the middle, 50-50, on this decisive question.[14]

Paradoxically, in order to best the formidable Willkie, FDR knew "that to win a third term, he would have to be the candidate best qualified to keep the country out of war. He would have to sell his emerging policy of peace through strength, to seek peace by preparing for war."[15] As the 1940 presidential election progressed, over this central campaign issue of foreign policy FDR had the support of 75 percent of the American people, a remarkable political accomplishment in such a complicated political situation.[16]

However, Willkie was not licked yet. Barnstorming more than 25,000 miles around the country, he found his political stride late in the contest. Though steadily behind for most of the campaign, he began to gain political traction by concentrating on his claim that Roosevelt was secretly determined to take America into the war. As Willkie thundered, "They [America's soldiers] are already almost at the boats!"[17] The gambit seemed to be working, as he closed the gap with FDR. A Gallup poll in late August 1940 showed Roosevelt only ahead of his rival by a whisker, 51 to 49 percent, within the margin of error.[18]

Willkie was surely right on the facts. Over the past several years, FDR had—slowly, and always in line with American public opinion—transformed America from an isolationist country into one capable of fighting Nazism in defense of primary US geostrategic interests. But Roosevelt was painfully aware the country was not prepared to take this final strategic step, and that Willkie was gaining political traction in pointing out the obvious. In painting himself as the peace candidate, while tarring FDR with the brush of being a warmonger, Willkie had at last found his issue.

Roosevelt—following his curious, idiosyncratic modus operandi of being tactically devious while strategically high-minded—was determined to stem Willkie's surge. The climax of the campaign was October 30, when FDR gave a speech saying, "I have said this before, but I shall say it again and again and again: Your boys are not going to be sent into any foreign wars."[19] And with this ringing declaration, FDR won himself a third term.

In his heart of hearts, Roosevelt almost surely knew his pivotal assertion was false. As far back as September 1939, FDR had told a group of senators that Hitler was "a nut."[20] Likewise, British political leader Clement Attlee, after a day out with Roosevelt on the presidential yacht in October 1941, would state, "He [FDR] had no illusions as to the nature of Nazism."[21] While he may have hoped, against the odds, that America could merely serve as the "Arsenal of Democracy," bankrolling London (and later Moscow) to victory while sparing his people the agony of war, FDR must have known this was likely a forlorn hope.

But the American people, though by now firmly on Britain's side against Hitler, were not ready in Roosevelt's view to stare into the abyss, seeing the consequences over the past few years as preparing the US for war. So, in the pursuit of saving the world, FDR—the American Sphinx—dissembled. And it worked. By late September, Gallup showed Roosevelt opening up a twelve-point lead.[22] New York's independent-minded Republican mayor, Fiorello La Guardia, caught the public mood in saying, "I would rather have FDR for all his known faults than Willkie with his unknown qualities."[23]

In the end, FDR bested Willkie in the 1940 presidential contest in a clear outcome. He won the race by a comfortable 5 million votes, or 10 percent of the American voter cohort. FDR received the same 27 million votes as in 1936, though Willkie had upped the Republican total to 22 million. The electoral college was more decisive, with Roosevelt gaining 449 electoral votes to Willkie's 82, even as FDR won thirty-eight states to Willkie's ten. The Democrats serenely remained the dominant force in the Congress, controlling the Senate 66-30 and the House 268-167.

By fair means and foul, Roosevelt had his mandate to propel America into the fulcrum of world affairs. But he was only able to do so because of his realist rationale for his policies: that the US would never be strategically safe if either Europe or Asia was subsumed by a hostile power.

Saving the British, saving the world

Once again, Roosevelt bestrode the American political scene like a colossus. A Gallup poll taken at the time of the third inauguration, in January 1941, found Roosevelt's popularity at a mighty 71 percent, higher than at any time since his first days as president.[24] He once again had won the American people's trust, securing the precious elixir of political legitimacy as he carried out his controversial, foreign policy high-wire act.

As Conrad Black asserts, FDR's triple challenge was to bring American public opinion along with him as quickly as he possibly could, to give the British as much wherewithal to continue the fight as he possibly could, and to rearm the US as quickly as he possibly could.[25] Only then would America be ready for the storm that was about to break upon it.

To put it mildly, this was a gargantuan strategic task. But Roosevelt began to turn the tide against the heretofore dominant isolationist impulse. For example, he recruited the 1936 Republican national ticket, Governor Alf Landon and Colonel Frank Knox, to his cause, as well as a highly respected GOP stalwart, former Secretary of State Henry Stimson. In June 1940, FDR shocked his rivals by naming Knox Secretary of the Navy and Stimson the powerful Secretary of War.* Learning from Woodrow Wilson's pigheaded refusal to broaden his political base, Roosevelt used such acts of bipartisanship to powerfully advance his realist, internationalist cause.

FDR was also lucky in his choice of enemies. Senator William Borah,[26] the aging Lion of Idaho and the totem of American non-interventionism, had severely damaged his credibility by his off-base predictions that war would never break out in Europe, made right up until the invasion of Poland.[27] Deeply diminished, he was to die in June 1940. Likewise, Colonel Charles Lindbergh—a national hero since making the world's first nonstop solo flight across the Atlantic, and perhaps the foremost celebrity of his day—proved to be as politically maladroit as Roosevelt was canny.

For instance, during a radio address on September 15, 1939, Lindbergh asserted that the primary goal of the US must be to "carry

---

* Today's Secretary of Defense.

on Western civilization"[28] by resolutely staying out of the war. Critically, Lindbergh implicitly denied any qualitative differences between the Nazis and the western democracies, a fact that became harder and harder to square as the extent of the German atrocities increasingly became clear. Polls at the time indicated that 84 percent of Americans were for Allied victory, while only 2 percent were rooting for the Nazis.[29]

Lindbergh, in his overt support for Nazism, was taking a disastrous course wholly at odds with the American public. In the process, he was discrediting the broader isolationist movement, which was generally not for the barbarous Hitler, but merely doubted that Germany could be stopped from winning the war.

Even the intellectual Senator Robert A. Taft of Ohio, who with the passing of Borah was now the primary foe of FDR in the Congress, announced his intention to support the president's efforts to bolster Britain and France. But, in the end, Lindbergh was by far his own worst enemy. He finished digging his political grave with a November 1939 article in *Reader's Digest*, which explicitly made his racist and pro-Hitler views clear. Political ruination rightly followed.

By October 5, 1941, Gallup polling indicated that an overwhelming 70 percent of Americans believed that it was more important to defeat Hitler than to stay out of the war.[30] In just a few short years, FDR's unparalleled political abilities had utterly changed America's perceptions about the world, going from being a country wholly against foreign intervention under any circumstances to one about the enter the most pivotal conflict in world history. However, the key to this seemingly revolutionary change was that Roosevelt, ever the political magician, was actually evolutionarily updating America's organic realist policy, in effect since the founding of the republic. FDR had turned the political tide and could now concentrate on helping a desperate Britain to survive.

Privately, Roosevelt agreed with many of his countrymen's skepticism about the UK's chances for survival; during this period, he rated them as no more than one in three.[31] Yet, as Black shrewdly notes, "It was one of the constants of Roosevelt's adult life that he was often engaged in counteracting the pessimism of others, about polio, economic depression, and world war."[32] Nor was FDR an initial fan of Churchill, who he had unsatisfactorily met once in 1918 (Churchill himself could not recall the encounter). As FDR let slip to the cabinet upon Churchill being made prime minister, "I supposed Churchill was the best man England had, even if he was drunk half the time."[33]

Yet, for all this very real skepticism, Roosevelt knew that the survival of Britain (and later the USSR) was central to his realist strategy. If they could be bankrolled, America might not have to fight at all. If this proved wrong, the longer they survived and the more Nazi casualties they inflicted were all to the good as America raced against time to rearm itself for the coming fight. Roosevelt's brilliant Lend-Lease initiative ended the "cash" portion of the "cash and carry" strictures the previous Neutrality Acts had placed upon him. Essentially, FDR's policy was that the US would lend Churchill whatever he needed, at no cost, and that London would simply repay the US by giving back what it had borrowed when it could.

As FDR effectively explained in basic common-sense terms during a December 16, 1940 press conference, "Suppose my neighbor's home catches fire and I have a length of garden hose four or five hundred feet away. If he can take my garden hose and connect it up with his hydrant, I may be able to help put out his fire. Now what do I do? I don't say to him before that operation, 'Neighbor, my garden hose cost me $15, you have to pay me $15 for it.' ... I don't want $15. I want my garden hose back after the fire is over ... If it goes through the fire all right, intact, without any damage to it, he gives it back to me and thanks me very much for the use of it."[34]

By making clear that the situation should be viewed in interest-based terms (my neighbor's house is on fire, which might spread to my own) rather than the immediate costs, FDR decisively swung American public opinion behind Lend-Lease.

Just after besting Willkie, on December 29, 1940, Roosevelt delivered one of his most famous "Fireside Chats" to the American people, on the theme of the country serving as the world's "Arsenal of Democracy." A record 75 percent of the fearful US populace listened to the president over the radio or later read Roosevelt's remarks.[35] The speech was a monumental political success, with telegrams running 100-1 in the president's favor.[36]

Senator Taft mightily tried to rally support against Lend-Lease, criticizing its central concept by cleverly saying, "Lending war equipment is a good deal like lending gum. You don't want it back."[37] But by now, he was swimming against the political tide. On February 8, 1941, Lend-Lease cleared the House, 260-165, with the Senate approving on March 8, 60-31, largely along party lines.

After the House supported the Senate version of the Lend-Lease bill, the very next day Congress appropriated $7 billion to fund the first arms shipments to the UK, the largest single appropriation up until then made in US history. America, due to Roosevelt's realist urgings, was now wholly committed to supporting the defense of Britain. As ever, the eloquent Churchill had the best line about Lend-Lease. Speaking in parliament, he called it "the most unsordid act in the history of any nation."[38]

In promoting his Lend-Lease initiative to help Britain, FDR could then hand over practically unlimited amounts of arms and materiel to London. In the end, more than $50 billion would be dispensed by the US under Lend-Lease agreements up until the end of the war. To give one an idea of the role resupply played in World War II, it is a startling fact that, apart from tanks, the British army was miraculously rearmed (largely by the US) within six months after retreating from Dunkirk in June 1940.[39] But what Lend-Lease really amounted to was enlightened realism.

Then, electrically, on June 22, 1941, Hitler made things immeasurably worse for himself, invading Stalin's Russia with 180 divisions. Operation Barbarossa left Stalin, Churchill, and Roosevelt as highly unlikely bedfellows. Despite his antipathy for Bolshevism, FDR moved quickly to support Stalin's desperate efforts to fend off the Nazi onslaught. In classic realist terms, Roosevelt "reasoned that Hitler was the primary enemy and that it was illogical to withhold aid to the country that would inflict most of the casualties on the Germans because its regime was distasteful."[40]

By making decisive strategic realist choices, FDR's America correctly saw that the threats to American interests emanating from Nazism and communism had a different time frame; they could be dealt with sequentially rather than concurrently. As such, the old realist adage, "The enemy of my enemy is my friend," came into play for FDR. He quickly moved to include Moscow in future Lend-Lease appropriations, a bold policy move that paid decisive strategic dividends as the USSR endured ten times as many casualties fighting Nazism as did the British and Americans combined.[41]

The final piece of Roosevelt's strategic puzzle involved America's breakneck efforts not only to supply arms for the anti-Nazi world, but also to prepare to enter the war itself. This was an obvious economic win-win for the administration, as "World War II had enabled Roosevelt to conclude the New Deal in glorious victory."[42] It is hard to overstate the economic jumpstart the war provided for the American economy. For example, US steel output in 1941 was a whopping 125 percent of the combined production of Germany, the USSR, Great Britain, and Japan. This dominance was repeated or exceeded in every category of strategic manufacturing, from aircraft to shipping.[43] The war didn't only definitively end the Depression. It also ushered in a new era of American economic preeminence.

Men had to be matched to all this new US military wherewithal. As was true with his foreign policy, FDR moved gingerly toward instituting the draft, never getting too far ahead of his worried countrymen. At the time of France's surrender to Hitler in June 1940, just slightly more than half of Americans polled favored the draft. A year later, in July 1941, after Roosevelt's discreet urgings, a decisive 69 percent favored the selective service. By August that figure stood at a towering 86 percent as the clouds of war darkened.[44]

A key reason for this decisive support was that FDR persuaded Wendell Willkie, his gallant presidential opponent in 1940, to come out publicly in support of the draft. Once again learning from the negative lessons of arrogant, disastrous Woodrow Wilson, FDR strove to make his foreign policy as bipartisan as possible, reaping the predictable political reward of such a tactic. The first peacetime draft in US history came into effect on September 16, 1940. Just a month later, American men 21–35 years old began to sign up.

Roosevelt's overall foreign policy was as strategically bold as it was tactically nimble. As Kissinger sagely notes, "In less than three years, Roosevelt had taken his staunchly isolationist people into a global war. As late as May 1940, 64 percent of Americans had considered the prospect of peace more important than the defeat of the Nazis. Eighteen months later, in December 1941, just before the attack on Pearl Harbor, the proportions had been reversed—only 32 percent favored peace over preventing [Hitler's] triumph."[45]

By then, against great political odds, FDR had decisively shaped American foreign policy, by siding with the British, serving as the world's "Arsenal of Democracy," and galvanizing the country to join the maelstrom itself. As Kissinger grandly puts it, "Roosevelt was able to persuade a society which had for two centuries treasured its invulnerability of the dire perils of an Axis victory."[46] But he had managed this near-miracle because the rationale for such a shift was beguilingly organic and traditional: his adherence to American realism.

The Japanese solve FDR's last problem

Meanwhile, a world away from Roosevelt's preoccupation with Nazi efforts toward the domination of the European portion of the Eurasian landmass, another aggressive great power was in increasingly dire straits. Imperial Japan, at war in China since 1937, had bogged down. While the ambitions of its militaristic government were as great as those of its Nazi ally—it wished to dominate Asia even as Germany coveted the whole of Europe—its ability to do so had already been exposed as wanting.

Worse, its economic dependence on America was forcing Tokyo to make a fateful choice: either it had to back down and humiliatingly abandon its efforts to dominate the Indo-Pacific or it had to boldly strike at its US tormentor and go for broke, hoping that quick conquests could make up for its glaring lack of domestic raw materials. Despite the long odds, given that Japan is nothing if not an honor culture, and that a climb-down would surely mean the end of the military controlling Japanese politics, its leadership opted to double down on war.

Japan was dependent on US oil for a decisive 78 percent of its needs. It consumed an estimated 12,000 tons of oil each day and had less than a two-year supply on hand.[47] Due to brutal Japanese aggression in China, these critical exports had been drastically cut back by the US administration in the summer of 1940. America's foot was now firmly on Imperial Japan's windpipe.

The oil embargo on Japan had become US policy almost as an afterthought. Assistant Secretary of State Dean Acheson, a Japan hawk, had somewhat unilaterally (and imperiously) imposed the ban, after which FDR ignored the warnings of Cordell Hull, his Secretary of State, and Sumner Welles, his Under Secretary of State—as well as the State Department's Asia hands—that such a policy would directly lead to war. Instead, FDR accepted the ban as settled American policy. Why would the adroit Roosevelt behave in such a cavalier fashion, ignoring the warnings of Acheson's superiors and a host of Asia experts?

Obviously, the wily American Sphinx knew what he was doing. Privately speaking to Canadian prime minister Mackenzie King in November 1941, FDR bluntly told him that any request he made of the Congress for a declaration of war against Germany would be defeated.[48] The country was still psychologically not ready. Later, at Yalta in 1945, Roosevelt told both Churchill and Stalin "that without a direct attack on American territory he 'would have had great difficulty getting the American people into the war.'"[49] In the weeks just prior to the Pearl Harbor attack, a poll showed that almost 75 percent of Americans remained opposed to another war with Berlin.[50]

So, the historical record makes it clear that it was FDR's view that the US would only go to war if it was directly attacked. To lure the Germans into such a trap, Roosevelt became more and more provocative in the Atlantic. He was ordering armed naval convoys to protect the war supplies the US was sending to Britain, tiptoeing right up to the line of participation in the conflict itself, all the while hoping Berlin would take the bait and attack US shipping, much as had led to American participation in World War I. But for all this, and despite some incidents at sea, the Germans did not take the bait.

This explains FDR's otherwise inexplicable policy toward Japan. "Roosevelt knew perfectly well the consequences of turning these screws [the oil embargo]; Japan would give up her territorial ambitions or attack."[51] Roosevelt banked on the cast-iron reality that "Japan was not going to withdraw from China and the US was not going to relax the embargo until she did."[52] The outcome could only be war.

While this does not mean that Pearl Harbor is a conspiracy theorist's dream, "Roosevelt acquiesced knowingly in a policy that would result in a Japanese attack on the West."[53] As Black precisely puts it, "Although he did not know where or exactly when Japan would strike, Roosevelt returned to Washington on the night of December 6 sure, but unperturbed, that for him and his country, war was finally imminent."[54]

* * *

Attack finally came at Pearl Harbor, at 7:48 a.m. on December 7, 1941. The Imperial Navy of the Empire of Japan, attacking without warning as it had done in the Russo-Japanese War in the early days of the twentieth century, unleashed itself against the US Pacific Fleet, serenely docked in Hawaii that Sunday morning. In two devastating waves over a ninety-minute period, 353 Japanese fighters, bombers, and torpedo planes swooped down, launched from six Japanese aircraft carriers.

The damage was immense. All eight US battleships docked at Pearl were struck, and four of them sunk. The Japanese attack destroyed 188 aircraft (the vast majority of them on the ground, having never even made it into combat), while 2,400 Americans were killed and 1,200 wounded. Japanese losses were negligible. At the same time, Tokyo struck the US-controlled Philippines, Guam, and Wake Island, and the British in Malaya, Singapore, and Hong Kong.

Strategically, the lightning attack amounted to a preventative action to neutralize the Pacific Fleet, keeping it from interfering with Japan's coming military penetration into Southeast Asia, particularly the resource-rich Dutch East Indies and Malaya. This is where Tokyo sought desperately necessary oil and rubber to maintain its military might, given the US oil embargo.

Pearl Harbor amounts to a true hinge point of history. As I put it in *To Dare More Boldly*, "The Japanese attack on the central American naval base at Pearl Harbor changed the course of the war fundamentally, drawing in America as the decisive force which altered the correlation of power around the world."[55] This is less due to the attack itself, and more to the momentous diplomatic and political forces it triggered.

First, the attack destroyed the credibility of isolationism forever and led to a basic reorientation of US foreign policy. As Senator Arthur Vandenberg, a key Republican on the Senate Foreign Relations Committee and a former isolationist, put it, "The day [Pearl Harbor] ended isolationism for any realist."[56] Two hundred years of successfully relying on the moats that were the Atlantic and Pacific oceans to protect primary American interests had come to an end. Now it was Roosevelt's new realist geopolitical doctrine—the Roosevelt Rule, that America must never let any competing great power dominate either portion of the primary Eurasian landmass—that replaced this outmoded view. The world had grown smaller, but it was still a realist one.

Second, Pearl Harbor united America as never before. No previous American war had anything like the unanimous domestic political support that the Japanese attack afforded Roosevelt. FDR's declaration of war resolution unanimously passed the Senate, 82-0, and overwhelmingly passed the House, 388-1. The president had what he needed to defeat Japan in all the hard days to come: a passionately united country. As Kissinger states, "By initiating hostilities, the Axis powers had solved Roosevelt's lingering dilemma about how to move the American people into the war."[57]

Third, the attack caused the Nazis to commit diplomatic suicide, just as FDR had dreamed. Neither Hitler nor Mussolini had been told about Pearl Harbor before the attack by their Japanese allies. The fascist Tripartite Pact made it clear that they were under no obligation to follow Japan's lead and take on the US. The terms of the agreement stated specifically that their militaries agreed to help Japan only if it was attacked by a third power; it said nothing about what happened if Tokyo was the aggressor.

Yet, on December 11, 1941, Germany declared war on the US, getting FDR out of a very tight strategic spot, for it would have been very hard for him to convince Congress to declare war on a country that had not directly done anything to America. Given the magnitude of his blunder, Hitler's reasons for declaring war on the US seem in retrospect laughably slight.

First, he thought the US was about to declare war on Germany, anyway. It seemed better to beat FDR to the punch and show loyalty to his Japanese ally. Second, personally aware of the strategic difficulties in fighting a two-front war himself, Hitler felt the US would have great trouble doing so, as had he. Third, Japan, which after all had physically attacked the US at Pearl Harbor, would likely be the focus of Washington's efforts. Fourth, it would surely take America until 1943–4 to enter the war in a big way, giving Germany time to complete its conquest in Russia.

Of course, all of these calculations proved to be wrong, dooming Nazi Germany to destruction. As I put it in *To Dare More Boldly*, "The simple truth is that Hitler, vastly underestimating the endless productive capacity of the United States, didn't think declaring war on America mattered all that much."[58]

But of course, in the end, American participation in World War II was decisive. Roosevelt's painstaking, central part in preparing the US for such a role on its own makes him one of the greatest of American presidents. In the course of just over a week (December 5–11, 1941), the course of the war was decided. First, Stalin halted the German drive in Operation Typhoon at the last possible moment at the gates of Moscow. Second, the Japanese attack on Pearl Harbor at last caused the US to enter the war. Third, Hitler ensured the defeat of Nazi barbarism by catastrophically declaring war on America. But it was Roosevelt—the American Sphinx, the puppet master—who behind the scenes facilitated many of these great strategic changes. The man stricken with polio had come not just to save himself; he also saved the world.

What the Roosevelt Rule means for today

If realism holds that wars should only be rarely fought, and then only when primary US national interests are at stake, the Roosevelt Rule makes it clear what these primary interests consist of. At base, no single competing great power must be allowed to acquire control of either Europe or Asia, the two portions of the great Eurasian landmass that dominates our planet in terms of population and resources. Even the mighty Western Hemisphere, where American power remains dominant, is but an island off Eurasia. Much as British foreign policy for centuries centered on keeping Europe from coming under the thrall of any one opposing continental power, so modern realism in the form of FDR's rule dictates that American primary interests are as simple to explain as they are eternally challenging to defend.

The consequences of using Roosevelt's Rule in our own age are profound. For example, Russia—a declining great power with a puny GDP the size of the state of Texas; an aging, corrupt gas station with nuclear weapons—has shown it is no threat to take over Europe. Indeed, it cannot even take over Ukraine. As such, in realist terms, the Ukraine war is surely not a primary US interest. It is a sideshow that is dangerously draining away American resources and money from the Indo-Pacific, where resides most of the world's future economic growth as well as most of its future political risk.

For if the Roosevelt Rule holds that Ukraine is a third-order priority, it also makes it apparent that American competition with peer superpower China in the Indo-Pacific, particularly over Taiwan, amounts to a first-order American interest. After all, China's clear aim is to dominate the whole of Asia. A China in control of Taiwan and dominant in the Indo-Pacific would achieve that. We simply cannot allow that to happen or the Roosevelt Rule would be broken, ultimately leaving us living in a Chinese-dominated era.

Thankfully, Xi Jinping has bullied most of his neighbors, forcing them into America's arms. The United States must do everything it can to secure these regional allies. Increasing military deterrence and cementing local alliance ties are by far the best way to limit the chances of another war with a Pacific empire.

Roosevelt's greatness lay in his unique and uncanny ability to see through the thicket of current events, and to instinctively grasp the essential. Now, as then, as the Roosevelt Rule makes plain, America's primary geopolitical interest is in no hegemon emerging in Eurasia. We must grasp this central foreign policy reality if we are to successfully make our way through the daunting challenges that our new era poses.

~ 6 ~

AN AMERICAN FOREIGN
POLICY FOR AMERICANS

*Eisenhower takes on the permanent
war establishment*

A curiously underrated legend

It is safe to say that, by the time he was elected the 34th President of the United States in 1952, Dwight David Eisenhower was already a living legend. During his own lifetime, the five-star general who vanquished the Nazis was at the same time the most famous and popular man in the world, all the while remaining almost entirely personally unknowable. His many job titles and nicknames uncannily point out this curious paradox: "Ike," "The Hero of Normandy," "The Liberator of Europe," "The Boss," and finally, simply, "The President." The Olympian titles took Eisenhower out of the realm of the living, making him more marble than man.

Of course, there was a human side to Ike. Like many famous generals in American history (Washington and Lee come to mind), he spent much of his life successfully trying to govern a ferocious temper. On the other hand, he innately exuded a cheerful, sunny, can-do attitude that endeared him to both his military and his political superiors, and then to the world as a whole. Ike fit comfortably into the Midwestern tradition of how a man of his time should behave: kindly yet hard, decent yet quietly competitive, approachable yet emotionally reserved.

Brilliant at poker, an expert bridge player, Eisenhower was superficially gregarious and social. A sportsman all his life (in his youth he had played running back at West Point, while as an older man he famously adored golf), Eisenhower was also an outdoorsman, drawn to fishing, hunting, and other solitary pursuits. After being cajoled into it by Churchill, the general became an avid painter (another solitary hobby), finishing several hundred quite all right, if conventional, canvases in his later life.

But while always being enormously popular, and with the whole of America behind him in what amounted to a twenty-year love affair (he was voted Gallup's "Most Admired Man of the Year" twelve times, still more than anyone else), almost no one knew what was behind the affable grin, the optimistic aura of easy command, and the resonant, authoritative voice that resembled nothing so much as Clark Gable's. Upon his death, his wife, Mamie, was asked who knew her husband best. She cannily replied, "No one."

This dual trait of being utterly recognizable and yet enigmatically unknowable initially did not serve Eisenhower's memory well. Just after his eight-year tenure in the White House came to an end—when Eisenhower, who was the oldest president ever at the time (at seventy), was succeeded by the glamorous youngest elected president, JFK (at forty-three)—historians ranked him in the bottom third of all chief executives, about level with the forgettable Chester Arthur.

In the early 1960s, at the height of youth-worshipping Camelot, the former president was seen as an amiable, do-nothing duffer, a man who had not let running the country get in the way of his golf game (this despite the fact that JFK played golf more often, and better, than Ike did). The 1950s came to be seen as a time of stagnation, an era when early chances for advances in civil rights and the search for an accommodation with the Soviet Union were squandered. Eisenhower's administration was initially viewed by many, generally left-leaning, historians as a wasted opportunity.

With the passage of time, this early, almost entirely incorrect historical caricature of Eisenhower as having turned the White House into "the tomb of the well-known soldier" has been dramatically replaced. A new consensus has formed of an administration and a man who skillfully steered the country through the early shoals of the Cold War, following realist precepts of foreign policy restraint, inaugurating an era of unprecedented peace and prosperity. Eisenhower has correspondingly shot up the presidential charts and is now seen by a majority of historians as a successful, underrated chief executive. That is as it should be but it is not nearly enough.

For the successful decade that Eisenhower bequeathed to the nation was not the result of luck, or even merely tactical adroitness. Behind the "hidden hand presidency,"[1] as Eisenhower's behind-the-scenes style came to be known, lurked coherent realist precepts, thinking, policies, and ideals; essential inputs that drove the highly favorable outcome that was America in the 1950s. This "Eisenhower Way" has been forgotten, just as the real man behind the grin has so often eluded the grasp of a series of first-rate biographers.

For, lurking beneath his highly appealing facade, Eisenhower was also an unlikely first-rate thinker, one whose innovative foreign and domestic policies did nothing less than to set the United States on course for victory in the Cold War, ushering in an unprecedented eight years of peace and prosperity. We must rediscover this misunderstood giant, rescuing him from an undeserved intellectual obscurity. Eisenhower's brilliant foreign and domestic policy must be studied and adopted by the United States today if we are to save our world and our country, as Ike so adroitly rescued his.

Saving the Republican Party and securing Cold War victory

The 1952 Republican presidential nomination fight, where an initially reluctant Eisenhower was induced by a grassroots movement to run for and ultimately win the prize, was one of the most consequential yet obscure political events of the twentieth century. Eisenhower, with his long fascination for classical history, had a true aversion to famous generals running for high political office, fearing—as American founders such as Thomas Jefferson had—that such a road could lead directly to Caesarism, and the end of republics. This unease was why he privately spoke scathingly of General MacArthur's endless political ambitions, and made it clear in 1948 (when the presidency was his for the asking) that he would not be running for the White House.

But by 1952, Ike had dramatically changed his mind. Convinced by Republican stalwarts of its moderate East Coast establishment—such as former Governor of New York Thomas Dewey and Senator Henry Cabot Lodge of Massachusetts*—that he alone could save the soul of the GOP in terms of its foreign policy orientation, Eisenhower, despite great misgivings, allowed his name to be put forward as a presidential candidate for the party.

The personification of all this unease was Senator Robert A. Taft of Ohio. The scion of one of the most famous families in American political history (his father had uniquely been both president and Supreme Court chief justice, and his grandfather Secretary of War), Taft was known as "Mr. Republican," being the acknowledged leader of the conservative Old Guard of the party and the favorite of much of the GOP's base. In many ways, Taft was unambiguously a great man. One of the smartest men in America—he had finished first in his class at Yale and at Harvard Law School—Taft's grasp of policy and legislation was second to none. Erudite, brave, incorruptible, a committed patriot, Taft was later named one of the five most important men ever to serve as a United States senator.

But for Eisenhower and his backers, Taft being able just meant that he was more dangerous. For while the two men agreed about much in terms of domestic policy, over foreign affairs they were light years apart.

---

* Yes, another Cabot Lodge. He was the grandson of his formidable namesake, who we met in Chapter 4.

For Senator Taft did not believe that Stalin's Russia was a major problem: poor, devastated by World War II, and thousands of miles away. For him it was a minor irritant to the US and not an existential threat to the American way of life.

Senator Taft's fears were not about Stalin, but about what would happen to America itself if an arms race were started with the Soviets. Echoing Eisenhower, Taft was always on the lookout for the increased militarization of the American republic, fearing not only economic ruin but also that, in such a climate of massive rearmament, war would become a self-fulfilling prophecy. While Eisenhower entirely agreed with the senator that the military-industrial complex had to be guarded against, he also saw the Soviets as a real threat, and one which needed to be actively resisted. It was the accurate dual-headed nature of the dangers ahead for America in the Cold War that Eisenhower, rather than the isolationist Taft, clearly discerned.

Eisenhower and his adherents pointed out that Taft's philosophy had been proven disastrously wrong once before. Ahead of Pearl Harbor, Taft had vigorously endeavored to keep America out of the coming war. Churchill's Britain must not be helped, in Taft's view, as doing so would only antagonize the soon-to-be victorious Nazis. Instead, the US must build up its navy and air force, and use the drawbridge of the Atlantic and Pacific oceans that surrounded it to withdraw from a Nazi-dominated world.

Eisenhower, as perhaps the preeminent military planner of his generation, had seen the basic, crippling flaw in Taft's strategic logic. Echoing the thinking of the Roosevelt Rule, Eisenhower saw that by withdrawing from the world, leaving Churchill and Stalin to their fates, the US would be effectively ceding Europe to the Nazis and Asia to the Japanese. But, as geographically the United States (and indeed the Western Hemisphere) is merely an island off the main Eurasian landmass, over time such an isolationist strategy would mean effectively ceding control of the world to what Churchill rightly described as the barbaric forces of darkness.

Given the overwhelming manpower and resources concentrated in Eurasia, a world run by Nazi Germany and Imperial Japan could be the only long-term outcome. The ill-conceived Japanese attack on Hawaii rescued Taft and the other isolationists of the time from moving ahead with their catastrophic policy advocacy. Now Ike could see that Taft was about to make the exact same strategic mistake with Stalin, all over again.

War-battered Western Europe was ripe for the Soviet plucking. In the face of such American timidity, the Soviets (and their Chinese communist allies) would soon come to dominate the whole of Asia as well. And a communist-dominated Eurasia would eventually mean its global triumph and American tragedy. Eisenhower had to act, saving the Republican Party (and the country) from such a calamity.

Before Eisenhower's decision to throw his hat into the political ring, Taft had been the clear Republican front-runner. Sixty-two at the time of the 1952 Republican race, despite his many attributes, the senator did enter the campaign with more than a few liabilities. Bespectacled, owlish, an uninspiring public speaker at best, and seemingly a cold fish, Taft lacked the people skills of such compatriots as the charming Franklin Roosevelt, or even the doughty Harry Truman. Compared with Eisenhower's movie-star glamor, the earnest, quiet Taft tended to melt into the background.

These personal differences helped seal the outcome of their political battle. For the Republican Party had not won the presidency since far-off 1928. Given their deepest desires, the conservative Republican Old Guard (and even the party base) may well have personally preferred Taft to Ike. However, more than this, they wanted to win. And with General Eisenhower as their standard-bearer, the long Republican sojourn in the political wilderness would at last come to an end.

The fight for the Republican presidential nomination in 1952 ended up being one of the closest and most bitter in American history. In an age where primaries were still the exception (party bosses at the political conventions tended to control things, with their deliberations proving decisive in terms of the nominee), of twelve open primary contests, Eisenhower won five and Senator Taft the same number, with the other two states going to minor candidates. Heading into the Chicago convention of July 1952, the race was seen as too close to call.

But Eisenhower's moderate backers still had an ace up their sleeve. They charged that the Taft campaign (especially in Texas and other southern states where the senator's support was strongest) had underhandedly refused to reserve a portion of their delegate slots for the Eisenhower team, instead putting the senator's backers in their place. Senator Taft, a man of the highest rectitude, angrily denied the charge, but he was forced to accede in allowing the convention to vote on the matter.

The initial delegate count was intensely close, with Eisenhower at 595 delegates and Taft just behind with 500. However, putting forward their "Fair Play" proposal on the very first day of the convention, Eisenhower's allies Dewey and Lodge demanded that a portion of the Taft supporters be evicted as delegates, and that the general's adherents be installed. The Fair Play proposal passed on the floor of the convention by the close vote of 658-548, with Taft losing a significant portion of his southern delegate tally; in the end the Texas delegation voted 33-5 for Eisenhower. Following this sea change, the large, uncommitted delegations in Michigan and Pennsylvania swung behind the general, sealing the nomination for Ike, who won on the first ballot, 845 delegates to 280.

It was here that Eisenhower showed the subtle leadership skills that would make him such a first-rate president. Aware of the bad blood between the two Republican camps, Eisenhower broke with precedent and went to see Senator Taft in his hotel suite in Chicago to personally ask him for his support, as a sign of respect. In the autumn of 1952, just before the November election, fearing Taft's supporters might not come out to vote in the contest, Eisenhower went to visit Taft again, this time in New York City. A very public show of unity was held before the cameras, following a private deal where Eisenhower agreed that there would be no future reprisals against Taft supporters should he become president, and that he concurred with Taft that federal spending should be cut.[2]

While Eisenhower was ready to accommodate "Mr. Republican" over domestic matters (where they largely agreed), what he did not concede to the senator is far more important. Eisenhower did not give way on his central insistence that the Republican Party should now support his internationalist position on foreign affairs, rather than either the isolationism of Taft or the brinksmanship of General MacArthur. It was in defeating Taft that Eisenhower truly saved the Republican Party, and perhaps the country, from itself during the Cold War era.

Ike's sunny charm quickly won the taciturn senator over, and by April 1953 they were increasingly close friends and even golfing buddies. Senator Taft, now the new Senate Majority Leader, became a champion of Eisenhower's domestic policy and crucially smoothed the way for a rapprochement between the conservative Old Guard of the party and Eisenhower's more moderate supporters. Taft's untimely death from pancreatic cancer in July 1953 deprived Eisenhower of a crucial ally, and America of one of its most historically important senators.

But he had lived long enough to acquiesce in Eisenhower uniting the party, crucially around an internationalist foreign policy. Eisenhower successfully remade the GOP in his image over foreign policy issues, giving new life to a party that had lost the previous five races for the presidency. In winning, Eisenhower was seeing off his party's Old Guard and its isolationist impulses.

President Truman had earlier made the centrist Containment Doctrine the primary strategic concept defining the brewing American rivalry with the Soviet Union—the US would politically compete with the USSR, all the while eschewing the far-right Rollback Doctrine of direct military conflict with the Soviet Union, as well as far-left efforts to appease Stalin's adventurism.

In prevailing over his extremist foes—General Douglas MacArthur on the right and former vice president Henry Wallace on the left—the Truman White House had temporarily secured Containment as the keystone of America's Cold War foreign policy. Instead of either accommodation or war, political competition with the Soviets was to be the modus operandi of the Truman years. But this fragile, temporary intellectual and political victory would have amounted to nothing if the Republican Party had not also come to adopt Containment thinking as its own.

While in the immediate postwar period Eisenhower had been remarkably dovish toward his wartime allies the Soviets (he and Russian marshal Georgy Zhukov became good friends), by mid-1947—following the rise in East–West tensions over economic recovery in Germany and the Greek civil war—Eisenhower came to agree with President Truman's Containment policy to stop Soviet aggression.

By politically vanquishing the isolationist Taft (and then early in his term prevailing over restive bureaucratic forces in his own administration through the 1953 Project Solarium war game exercise), Eisenhower made all the difference, cementing the Containment Doctrine as the foreign policy strategy of both major American political parties throughout the long Cold War to come.

The bipartisan nature of the support for Containment allowed the strategy to survive the coming myriad changes in US political fortunes, acquiring a continuity rarely seen in any democratic great power's foreign policy. It is the miraculous political staying power of Containment that led America to eventual victory in the Cold War. This remarkable foreign-policy intellectual durability would simply not have come about without Eisenhower's pivotal victory over Taft in the 1952 Republican presidential race.

A record of restraint

It was in Eisenhower's practical policy success in ending the Korean War that his earlier efforts to champion Containment as America's foreign policy strategy came to fruition. Disdaining the pleas of his former mentor General MacArthur that America had to escalate the war (by the dropping of 30–50 atomic bombs on Manchuria) to reclaim North Korean territory via Rollback, as well as of far-left appeasers who felt the US had no need to stand up to communist aggression in the first place, Eisenhower predictably charted a middle course.

MacArthur had famously proclaimed that "in war there can be no substitute for victory."[3] In favoring a far more restrained policy on the Korean peninsula, Eisenhower was to answer, "Yes, there is. The substitute is holding the line and preventing the enemy from winning." Eisenhower's successful ending of the Korean War and the dawning of the nuclear age made it clear that the United States no longer lived in the World War II era of all-or-nothing certainties. It was the very changed nature of this new age that made it clear that the president's advocacy of limited war made eminent sense, even as the new world left former giants such as MacArthur intellectually behind.

In late 1952, the president-elect visited Korea to get a first-hand feel for the situation. Eisenhower had campaigned on the nebulous promise that he would "go to Korea," implicitly reassuring the American people that the military stalemate that had developed there over the past two years could be brought to a quick end. Given the ideological stakes at play, it was absolutely vital that Ike end the Korean War on politically successful terms if his centrist Containment Doctrine were to gain traction and permanence with the American people.

Chairman Mao was quick to test the new president's resolve. As Eisenhower came to power, Mao's Chinese communist army in North Korea began a military build-up in the Kaesong sanctuary. But Eisenhower was not to be bullied; he bluntly threatened Mao with the use of nuclear weapons if an armistice were not quickly concluded.

At this critical juncture, the new administration caught a strategic break. With the death of Stalin in March 1953, Russian support for Mao's hardline position on the Korean War evaporated as it turned inward for its succession struggle. With his ally heading for the door, Mao decided to compromise with the US over the outstanding issue of returning prisoners of war, the ostensible reason that peace talks had gone nowhere. With this diplomatic breakthrough, the Korean armistice was dramatically concluded in July 1953, just six months into Eisenhower's term.

The war left Korea divided into North and South along boundaries close to those that had prevailed before the conflict. In an implicit repudiation of the left's advocacy of appeasing Stalin, Eisenhower had successfully stood up to communist aggression, safeguarding South Korea. But on the other hand, in a rejection of the far right's advocacy of Rollback Doctrine, he had not continued an unpopular war in the vain and immeasurably dangerous hope of conquering North Korea through the use of atomic weapons.

Ironically, by threatening the then recalcitrant Chinese with the horrifying option of nuclear annihilation, Eisenhower had broken the diplomatic logjam, securing the successful end of the war and at the same time paradoxically buttressing his support for the centrist Containment Doctrine. Eisenhower's overall strategic goals centered around realism and restraint: avoiding war, containing communism, and preserving the booming US economy. The Eisenhower administration is a tale of both what it did and what it did not do; to its everlasting credit, it did not turn the Korean War into a world war.

Likewise, Ike avoided disaster over the French calamity at Dien Bien Phu. Early in 1953, Paris asked Eisenhower for support in battling the Viet Minh, the Vietnamese communists attempting to throw their French colonial rulers out of the country. Suspicious of both French and Viet

Minh motives and determined not to be drawn into a protracted colonial war, the president dispatched Lieutenant General John W. "Iron Mike" O'Daniel to Vietnam to assess the political situation as well as the quality of French forces there. O'Daniel did not like what he found.

In addition to O'Daniel's gloomy report, Chairman of the Joint Chiefs of Staff Matthew Ridgway presented a comprehensive account of what a successful invasion would entail: a massive American military deployment. This dissuaded Eisenhower from intervening on behalf of the French. Prophetically, President Eisenhower stated at a National Security Council (NSC) meeting that "the war [in Vietnam] would absorb our troops by the divisions"[4] and was not worth the perilous risk.

While the administration did provide Paris with bombers and non-combat personnel, the president was determined to limit American involvement in aiding the French. This was partly due to the exorbitant estimated cost to the US in terms of money and lives, but also due to the terrible public relations and moral example that supporting a retrograde colonial power would broadcast to the rest of the world.

As Cold War tensions increased, Eisenhower—even at the height of American global power—was acutely aware that his era was not one of unipolarity, where the world was ruled by merely one great power. Even beyond the obvious bipolar structure of the Cold War, where the US and the USSR vied for global dominance, the president was entirely cognizant that a non-aligned developing world—countries beyond the direct control of either Washington or Moscow—amounted to a third global force.

As such, standing as the most powerful of the anti-colonial powers was an asset of incalculable value for the US. Eerily, such a world structure has returned in our own era, as beneath the American and Chinese superpowers, the emerging world has remained studiously neutral over the war in Ukraine, and amounts to a decisive force that may well determine the ultimate outcome of the Sino-American competition.

For the US to decisively side with France in Vietnam, tipping the military balance in favor of the old, dying colonial order against national liberation movements across the globe, would unnecessarily have made an enemy of much of the world, amounting to a cataclysmic public relations defeat for the United States and a windfall for its Soviet enemies. As a country which itself had come into being through an anti-colonial struggle against Great Britain, America risked ceding vast swathes of international credibility in the developing world, all for highly marginal gains in Vietnam.

Once again, Eisenhower used the devious tactics of the "hidden hand presidency" to further American interests. Ike managed to avoid saying "no" to the French while at the same time not unduly harming America's reputation with the developing world. Ike favored subsequent French requests for military assistance, but only with conditions the president knew would be impossible for Paris to accept, like joint western action agreed in advance, and congressional approval of the sales. For the president understood that moral authority is not just a phrase for the weak; world opinion matters a great deal in terms of practical American strategic power.

Finally, when the French fortress of Dien Bien Phu was about to be overrun by the Viet Minh in May 1954, Eisenhower steadfastly refused to militarily come to its rescue, despite urgings from the Chairman of the Joint Chiefs of Staff and Vice President Nixon that America support the French with a huge air strike. However, in moves that would come back to haunt America, Eisenhower offered military and economic aid to the new Republic of South Vietnam, the pro-western state that emerged from the Geneva talks that ended French rule in the country.

Fatefully, in February 1955, Eisenhower dispatched the first American soldiers to Vietnam, serving as military advisers training the new South Vietnamese army. The commitment would grow to some 900 men by the end of Eisenhower's presidency. While Eisenhower was not the primary author of the Vietnam disaster for the US (that dubious honor must go jointly to Presidents Kennedy and Johnson), his half-in, half-out strategy in Southeast Asia was a fateful beginning to the catastrophic Vietnam War, one which severely tarnished America's standing in the developing world.

However, on its own, the Dien Bien Phu saga stands as a positive example of Eisenhower managing to maintain America's close allied relationship with a great European power (in this case, France), all the while steering a broadly anti-colonial course, one which mattered in the increasingly important developing world.

In 1956, over the Suez Crisis—where Great Britain, France, and Israel tried to subvert developing-world leader Gamal Abdel Nasser of Egypt by militarily seizing the recently nationalized Suez Canal—Eisenhower came down even more strongly on the side of the anti-colonialists, thereby securing America's position in much of the world that desired neither Soviet nor western primacy. Decades ahead of his time, Eisenhower presciently saw that international relations amounts to more than transatlantic relations.

Additionally, Ike avoided disaster over Quemoy and Matsu. Having just skillfully ended the Korean stalemate, in late 1954 Eisenhower was confronted by a further military crisis with Communist China as he strove mightily to avoid yet another war. The tiny (and strategically unimportant) islands of Quemoy and Matsu were Chinese Nationalist strongholds just off the coast of China's Communist mainland. America had committed itself to defending the Chinese Nationalist cause, centered in Formosa. In September 1954, as Mao's People's Liberation Army (PLA) began shelling the two islands, American hawks demanded that President Eisenhower intervene against the mainland, as Nationalist territory was now under attack.

By the close of the year, Eisenhower's military and foreign policy experts at the NSC, as well as the Joint Chiefs of Staff and the State

Department, had unanimously recommended to the president on no less than five occasions that he use nuclear weapons if necessary to defend Quemoy and Matsu. Thankfully, the level-headed Eisenhower refused to do so.

Once again, he used ambiguity as a tactic to support his clear strategic line against military interventionism. The president refused to be drawn on what sort of attack on Quemoy and Matsu would lead to US counter-retaliation, retaining for himself maximum freedom of maneuver. While Eisenhower refused to give into the American hawks' calls for military intervention, at the same time he made it clear to Mao that the Chinese shelling could not continue if he was to steer the US clear of war. The president staged military exercises off the coast of China and tested advanced nuclear weapons in Nevada. Ike even mused aloud that he saw no reason why nuclear weapons should not be used in furthering American strategic goals in the world, a public view dramatically at odds with his extensive private misgivings.

Ike's bluff with Mao worked. Within weeks, Communist China stopped shelling the islands, and within months the crisis subsided, in early 1955. In again charting a moderate diplomatic path—disdaining the hawks' call for war, while at the same time standing up to Mao's aggression—Eisenhower had averted an utterly unnecessary conflict. Just as with Dien Bien Phu, Eisenhower had championed a realist anti-interventionism, prudently avoiding war except as a strategic tool of last resort. Better still, he managed to confront communism, all the while securing peace.

Ike's realist restraint was linked to his understanding of the limits of American power. More than any other Cold War president, Eisenhower understood the role economics plays in a country's overall power base. His administration—despite both Cold War pressures and the need for national infrastructure—kept a tight lid on federal spending. During his eight years in the White House, the president managed to balance the federal budget three times, a record of fiscal discipline unsurpassed since the dawning of the modern presidency.

Calling himself a "progressive conservative" and his program "dynamic conservatism," Eisenhower was a Republican who balanced budgets, slashed military spending, and resisted communism without going to war. Such heresies should be encouraged again today in both parties, if fiscal sanity is to regain its vital role in American political life.

For Eisenhower, rightly, fiscal prudence was a moral issue. "We must avoid the impulse to live only for today, plundering for our own ease and convenience the precious resources of tomorrow. We cannot mortgage the material assets of our grandchildren without risking the loss of their political and spiritual heritage."[5] Such sound stewardship, while a deeply unfashionable virtue today, is a major component of the Eisenhower Way. It deserves to be unearthed again, if an increasingly decadent America is to save itself from itself.

Calming the Sputnik panic

As his presidency entered its twilight years, Eisenhower was once again confronted by a Red Scare. From the distance of six decades, it is hard to understand how the Soviet launch of a very primitive satellite serving no practical purpose could have stirred up so much fear in the American people. But Sputnik, which gave the Soviets great global prestige at the time, illustrated that soon the USSR—given its relative technological prowess— would be able to launch a missile with a nuclear weapon aboard. After Sputnik, the shocking notion that the US might well be losing the Cold War to the feared and hated Russians struck America like a thunderbolt.

Eisenhower, knowing that this fear was entirely ungrounded, tried to calm the country, as he was concerned the hysteria would jump-start the wasteful military arms race between the two superpowers. But for once, Ike's famed calm, reassuring manner did not do the trick. Despite correctly proclaiming that the overall military strength of the free world was decidedly greater than the communist countries', Sputnik-mania gripped America.

The Democrats, sensing a political opening at last, opened hearings on the "missile gap" in the Senate, spearheaded by the young, ambitious John F. Kennedy. Eisenhower knew what was coming; he feared not a missile gap, but a missile race, and that the military leadership and the Democrats would use the Sputnik crisis to demand ruinous military spending in order to compete with the Soviets over an entirely manufactured problem.

In the end, Eisenhower decided he would not let a good crisis go to waste. Instead, he skillfully used the Sputnik hysteria to push for the foundation of the National Aeronautics and Space Administration (NASA), a civilian agency directed to build up American technology in the service of space exploration.

In fostering American technological prowess through the creation of NASA, Eisenhower—in line with the construction of the Interstate Highway System and the St. Lawrence Seaway—was not averse to establishing large government projects that served the nation's interests. At the same time, the president fervently hoped that his actions would quell the Sputnik hysteria, enabling him to hold the line on defense spending, balance the budget, and limit the militarization of American society.

Due to both Eisenhower's NASA initiative and, mimicking Sputnik, the fact that the US soon launched its own satellite into space, the hysteria that the US had somehow fallen behind the USSR in terms of technological prowess began to abate. The president, through his preternaturally steady demeanor, calm use of actual objective facts, and championing of the NASA initiative, had turned the tide. However, after Sputnik, keeping control of defense spending became an ever-harder task for Eisenhower and all his successors.

Even though he was the last American president to be born in the nineteenth century, Eisenhower had a remarkably modern take on how the dawning nuclear age would affect the practice of diplomacy. Despite the fact that he himself—over both the Korean armistice and the Quemoy and Matsu crisis—was not above bluffing about the use of nuclear weapons, his private position about them was starkly bleak. Once, when attending a White House meeting as to how the dollar could be reestablished in the US following a Soviet nuclear strike, the president grimly joked, "Wait a minute, boys. We're not going to be reconstructing the dollar. We're going to be grubbing for worms."[6]

As far back as the end of World War II, Eisenhower—almost uniquely—had grave concerns about the American use of the atomic bomb to end the war with Japan. Later, he recalled he was against its use, because "Japan was already defeated and ... dropping the bomb was completely unnecessary, and secondly because I thought that our country should avoid shocking world opinion ... I disliked seeing the United States take the lead in introducing into war something as horrible and destructive as this new weapon."[7] After unleashing the genie of the nuclear age, it is clear that Eisenhower had great fears it could not be controlled.

US-Soviet tensions had risen following the Sputnik hysteria, and Ike was determined to test the proposition that the Cold War could be thawed. With Stalin's death, there was a perceived chance for a rapprochement with the Soviets. Dramatically, the president invited new (and relatively less murderous) Soviet paramount leader Nikita Khrushchev to visit both him and the United States. From his wartime experience, Eisenhower knew the value of personal diplomacy—that it was harder to hate a man theoretically once you had gotten to know him personally, and that from there, differing national interests could more calmly be discussed and agreements reached.

And indeed, as Eisenhower and the premier talked at the presidential retreat Camp David (named for the president's grandson), a thaw in tensions ensued. The USSR and the US agreed to attend a peace summit in Paris, where they were scheduled for the first time to talk about placing limits on nuclear weapons production. At the same time, Khrushchev consented to rescinding a Soviet ultimatum regarding embattled Berlin, significantly easing Cold War tensions. Secretly, the Soviet leader was also looking for a peace dividend. Following Khrushchev's American trip, he was able to cut 1 million men from the Soviet armed forces, in the interests of bolstering his economy.

What was then called "the Spirit of Camp David" amounted to the first American effort at détente with the Soviets—a recognition that, given the horrors of nuclear war, some effort at nuclear limitation was absolutely imperative. Even beyond this, as was proven true in the Berlin crisis, Eisenhower hoped that differing Soviet-American national interests could be better aligned. Poignantly, it had taken a soldier who knew the horrors of war to begin the search for a superpower peace.

Building on the Spirit of Camp David, the Soviet-American summit of May 1960 was premised on the startlingly ambitious idea that the Cold War itself could at last be brought to an end. However, tragically, it was not to be. The abject failure of Paris amounted to the great "what if" of the Eisenhower presidency, the lost chance that saw the Cold War freeze up again, this time to unprecedentedly dangerous levels during the Kennedy administration.

Ironically, its failure was a direct result of the U-2 spy plane crisis, the one time when Eisenhower's rightly famed reputation for credibility let him down. This aberration occurred at the worst possible moment, with the chance for peace beguilingly within reach. However, this greatest failure of the Eisenhower presidency does not negate all the man had done throughout his long career of service in making personal credibility a central tenet of the Eisenhower Way. Rather, this rare lapse merely confirms this virtue's absolutely central importance.

Ahead of the summit meeting, Eisenhower—as he had shown during the Sputnik crisis—(rightly) did not believe that the USSR was ahead of America in missile technology. However, it was also certainly true that he could negotiate in Paris with more confidence if he knew this to be a fact. Assured that the U-2 spy planes were too high-tech to ever be caught, the president authorized CIA chief Allen Dulles to send them over the USSR to determine the precise state of the Soviet missile program. The overflights were to stop on May 1, 1960, just ahead of the summit. On the last possible day, at the worst possible moment, Captain Francis Gary Powers's U-2 was shot down over Soviet airspace.

Assuming the pilot was dead (given that the U-2 flew at very high altitudes), the president approved a CIA cover story designed to make this potentially massive embarrassment go away, falsely saying a weather plane had strayed into Soviet airspace from Turkey. However, by May 5, Khrushchev charged a spy plane had been shot down over the USSR. But even here, he gave Eisenhower diplomatic cover, blaming Pentagon warmongers for attempting to sabotage the summit—but not Eisenhower, his partner in peace. Crucially, in what amounts to the single biggest mistake of his presidency, Eisenhower doggedly stuck with the false cover story.

Now the Soviet diplomatic trap snapped shut. Khrushchev released photos of the downed U-2 as well as announcing that Powers had been captured alive, severely compromising American credibility in general and Eisenhower's in particular. The president had long felt his personal integrity, laboriously built over decades, was his greatest diplomatic asset. Disdaining any further efforts to blame either underlings or other American institutions (the CIA suggested the president forcefully—and rightly—blame it for the debacle, in an effort to rescue the summit), President Eisenhower at last admitted the U-2 fiasco was entirely his fault. It was a noble thing to do and spoke to the president's personal fineness as a man. But it was also too late.

Faced with Eisenhower's frank admission of culpability, Khrushchev rescinded his earlier invitation—following on from his own successful trip to the US—for Eisenhower to visit the USSR. With the diplomatic Spirit of Camp David dead in the water after the U-2 incident, the Paris Peace

Summit became the next casualty. As Khrushchev later frankly admitted in his memoirs, from the time Francis Gary Powers was shot down, he was never fully in control of the Soviet negotiating posture. Russian hard-liners used the U-2 crisis to force a far more bellicose policy on the Soviet leader.

Everything Eisenhower had epitomized—prudence, patience, strategic skill, and credibility—had eluded him at the worst possible moment. At the summit in Paris, Eisenhower, in an effort to stop the public relations disaster from continuing, refused to apologize to Khrushchev for the U-2 flights. The Soviet premier, under great pressure from his own hawks, stalked out of the meeting.

The summit came to an inglorious conclusion, and with it, the first real chance for détente between the two superpowers of the Cold War. It was a terrible end to Eisenhower's highly successful presidency. However, the tragedy of the Paris Peace Summit does not refute the Eisenhower Way. To the contrary, it confirms it. The one time the president turned away from his own credo, the results were calamitous.

Saving America from itself: Eisenhower's Farewell Address

Following the razor-thin victory of his youthful critic John F. Kennedy in the 1960 presidential election, Eisenhower was leaving office as a disappointed man. Kennedy had risen to prominence in the Senate, castigating the United States for ignoring a missile gap that Ike knew simply did not exist. He complained to friends that all his work was about to be undone; that given this he should have spent the 1950s "having fun," instead of steering America through the dangerous early days of the Cold War.

Yet Eisenhower still had something of the greatest importance to say to his people. He urgently wanted to warn them of the perils of over-militarizing American society. Even when he first ran for president in

1952, Eisenhower had been critical of what he saw as the excessive military spending of the Truman administration. It was the Hero of Normandy who had campaigned on a platform of restrained military expenditure and the need for balanced budgets. As far back as his 1952 campaign platform, Eisenhower had included a harsh critique of unaccountable military expenditures as a danger to the stability and long-term growth of the American economy. For Eisenhower, economic strength really was the lodestar of overall national power.

Given his status as the greatest of war heroes and the intimate knowledge of the armed forces his unique biography had given him, the president saw military spending as part of this larger whole. For him, defense expenditures were simply a necessary evil in American life, a lingering economic drain and potential political danger that must be watched over with the greatest care.

Early on in his first term, Eisenhower had tried to alert the American people about these dangers. In his Cross of Iron speech of April 16, 1953—following on from the unexpected death of Stalin—in the starkest terms, Eisenhower likened arms spending to stealing from the people. Highlighting the backbreaking cost of continued tensions with the USSR, he noted that America faced not only strategic perils like the Korean War, but also an ongoing arms race that, if unchecked, could come to corrode American life itself.

As the president passionately explained, "Every gun that is made, every warship launched, every rocket fired, signifies, in the final sense, a theft from those who hunger and are not fed, those who are cold and are not clothed. This world in arms is not spending money alone. It is spending the sweat of its laborers, the genius of its scientists, the hopes of its children. The cost of one modern heavy bomber is this: a modern brick school in more than 30 cities ... This is not a way of life at all, in any true sense. Under the cloud of the threat of war, it is humanity hanging from a cross of iron."[8]

In invoking the earlier Cross of Gold speech of populist William Jennings Bryan, Eisenhower was attempting to make Americans see that the basic trade-offs involved in excessive military spending were robbing the country of the good life it had struggled so valiantly to attain in World War II. Eisenhower wanted to avoid an unsustainable security burden leading to economic disaster. He was listened to respectfully, but the speech did not move the needle of public opinion.

His basic insight that "we must achieve both security and solvency. In fact, the foundation of military strength is economic strength"[9] was overshadowed by a rise in Cold War tensions as his second term came to an end. Trying to hold the line, Eisenhower admonished his warlike Secretary of State, John Foster Dulles, that America's strategic defense was utterly dependent on its fiscal system. By the end of the 1950s, this common-sense advice was increasingly falling on deaf ears as the Cold War heated up.

Throughout his presidency, Eisenhower would engage in a long, twilight struggle against fanatical Cold War hawks whose zeal risked fiscal and social ruin for the country they were striving so hard to defend. Bookending the Cross of Iron speech, in the last minutes of his presidency, Eisenhower was determined to spread his prophetic warning once again.

Working with his brother Milton and chief speechwriter, Malcolm Moos, Eisenhower's Farewell Address was painstakingly constructed; in the end the speech went through fully twenty-one drafts. In what was to be his final word, his last public speech to the nation as president, Eisenhower went before the cameras on January 17, 1961, just days before John F. Kennedy was sworn in as the country's thirty- fifth president.

If the Cross of Iron speech had been designed to point out the fiscal perils of excessive defense spending, illuminating the real choice that had to be made between serving America's economic and social well-being and its military defense, in the Farewell Address the president made an even starker argument. Without necessarily meaning to, the "military-industrial complex"—and the foreign policy establishment that supported its drive to look upon every problem through the military lens—could come to dangerously skew American decision-making toward policies that involved its perpetuation, leading to endless American wars and all the foreign and domestic suffering that such a stance would bring about. National bankruptcy and political Caesarism would inevitably follow if this permanent war party took control.

As the president warned, "The conjunction of an immense military establishment and a large arms industry is new in the American experience ... We recognize the imperative need for its development. Yet we must not fail to comprehend its grave implications ... In the councils of government, we must guard against the acquisition of unwarranted influence, whether sought or unsought, by the military-industrial complex. The potential for the disastrous increase in misplaced power exists and will persist. We must never let the weight of this combination endanger our liberties or democratic processes. We should take nothing for granted."[10]

Echoing America's founders, Eisenhower—using the bully pulpit of the presidency as he had never done before—pointed out that any vastly powerful interest group like the military-industrial complex must be suspiciously and constantly monitored, as it would invariably promote policies that led to its own perpetuation. In other words, for a man who sells hammers, every problem is a nail. For the military-industrial complex, every diplomatic crisis would be looked at in terms of American interventionism first—and not last, as realists would have it.

Eisenhower wanted to defend the United States from the Russian military but also from the other extreme, that countervailing American military spending that could put the republic itself in jeopardy, placing the country on a permanent war footing. As an ethical realist, the president understood the value of the ancient Greek virtue of balance. Aware from his great love of history that republics traditionally have committed political suicide, being susceptible to the coming of a military Caesar,

Eisenhower fretted that an overly militaristic America might be headed down this old, doleful road.

Throughout his presidency, Eisenhower worried deeply about the nation becoming a garrison state. The fact that a famous general should have been so intellectually suspicious of security institutions—their practices and motives—is a tribute to Eisenhower's genius as a man. One last time, America's greatest twentieth-century military hero answered the call to duty, warning that it was an overemphasis on his lifelong profession that could lead to the undoing of the country he had served the whole of his adult life.

Given all that has happened since—Vietnam, Iraq, Afghanistan—surely Eisenhower's Farewell Address amounts to some of the best political risk analysis ever tendered. The valedictory speech was the most memorable farewell address since George Washington's. It was Eisenhower's gift to the nation, the summation of all that he had learned, reminding America that what makes it admirable is not its foreign conquests, but what it is.

The Eisenhower Way in the twenty-first century

Like a fine wine, Eisenhower's Farewell Address has just gotten better with age. In our own world of many great powers, pursuing an American foreign policy based on limits is no longer a luxury, it is a strategic imperative. This means the US must be wary of its foreign policy establishment—the handmaiden to Ike's military-industrial complex—a majority of whose members have never met a foreign intervention they didn't like. Jeffersonians and Jacksonians must go back to Eisenhower's wise view that America engaging in war is a last resort and not the first.

Instead, in line with Eisenhower's holistic thinking about America, the US must always balance its internal economic and social needs—which presently include a $32 trillion debt, creaky infrastructure, third-rate schools, a porous border, out-of-control inner-city crime, and a fentanyl crisis that killed over 100,000 people in 2022—against the imperative of having a strong defense. America cannot do everything.

We live in an age where choices simply have to be made. This is a time of great promise, but also one of limits. It is a time in need of grown-ups. We must revive Ike's optimistic, confident, can-do style, embracing the notion of America as a great power, one that remains the envy of the world, but also sees an America that must live within the limits of today's multipolar world.

Eisenhower presided at the zenith of US power in the 1950s, yet he was perpetually aware of the limits of that colossal strength. The Eisenhower Way's balanced view—internationalist and outward-looking but mindful of both limits and the trade-offs between the strategic defense of American interests and domestic and social goods—must be the once and future realist foreign policy of the Republican Party. President Dwight David Eisenhower's thinking saved his world; curiously enough, it can also save ours.

~ 7 ~

DEFENDING THE PRIMARY
INTERESTS OF AMERICA

*In the Cuban Missile Crisis, JFK shuts
out the noise and saves the world*

One second to midnight

It was the most dangerous moment in the history of the world. In October 1962, American U-2 spy plane flights over Cuba definitively uncovered the presence of soon-to-be-installed Soviet intermediate- and medium-range ballistic missiles on Fidel Castro's island. Despite both public and private assurances to the contrary, Nikita Khrushchev's regime was intent on secretly destabilizing the underlying political equilibrium of the Cold War world.

John F. Kennedy, the youngest man ever elected to the presidency, had been in office for only twenty rather ruinous months. While it is difficult to remember in retrospect, up until the autumn of 1962 his administration had largely been a litany of failures. The disastrous Bay of Pigs invasion, a CIA-sponsored plan to train 1,400 Cuban exiles to invade their imprisoned island and remove Castro, had been a bloody debacle.* A bruising encounter with Khrushchev in Vienna had been followed by the construction of the Berlin Wall. Kennedy's domestic agenda was bottled up in Congress. In fact, until that fateful autumn, the president himself wryly admitted that his White House did not yet have a single major policy accomplishment to its credit.

But this was about to dramatically change, as JFK—cool, analytical, cerebral, quietly confident, wise, and unhysterical—saved the world

---

*　1,200 of the 1,400 Cuban exiles were killed or captured.

from nuclear Armageddon. This was far from a preordained outcome. Soon after the missile crisis, JFK confided to Ted Sorensen, his principal speechwriter and a close aide, that he thought the odds of a nuclear war occurring had been "somewhere between one in three and even."[1] In fact, from all that we have learned about the crisis since, this assessment is too generous; the odds were almost certainly worse than even this.[2]

Given the monumental stakes, it is unsurprising that the fourteen handpicked advisers who made up the ExComm—the Executive Committee of the National Security Council, the primary political-risk deliberative body JFK established to deal with the crisis—gave him such terrible, contradictory advice. More than anything, as the White House tapes of their deliberations make clear, there was a lot of "noise" in the room, with confusion, fear, and anger understandably driving a lot of the discussions and assessments. It is also apparent that the young president was the calmest man in the room.

For JFK had a secret intellectual weapon: a realist understanding that—amidst all the noise and the myriad and conflicting moving parts of the crisis—core American national interests, designed to secure the American nation, should always drive its foreign policy. While others worried about more peripheral issues—the military hawks in the Joint Chiefs of Staff obsessed about driving Castro from power, while doves in the person of UN ambassador Adlai Stevenson stressed war must be avoided by kowtowing to the Soviets, whatever the drastic loss of strategic credibility to the United States—Kennedy alone clearly and consistently articulated what ought to be the primary national interests underlying US foreign policy moves: that the Soviet missiles must be removed from Cuba and nuclear war must be avoided.

Everything else was negotiable, and all tactics that moved America toward this policy outcome must be entertained. Strategically immovable, tactically flexible, JFK's single-minded pursuit of these simple, profound, fixed national interests in securing the American homeland was the beacon he used to navigate the ship of state through the most hair-raising moment in human history.

*   *   *

Short, stocky, blustering, accustomed to wearing ill-fitting suits, Nikita Khrushchev at times reveled in playing the role of the quintessential Russian peasant that he had long since ceased to be. For, in reality, Khrushchev was a shrewd operator, well aware of what he was doing. It is easy to see that, from the Soviet perspective, arming Cuba with nuclear missiles was an act of protecting its imperiled ally.

Even following the Bay of Pigs fiasco in April 1961, the Kennedy brothers continued to keep up the political pressure. Robert Kennedy, his brother's attorney general and overall consigliere, was put in charge of Operation Mongoose, sponsoring a CIA campaign of harassment and sabotage on the island, including efforts to assassinate Castro himself. While this all came to nothing, it alarmed Khrushchev that one of his prize global assets was in constant peril.

In July 1962, Khrushchev reached a secret agreement with Castro to place Soviet nuclear missiles on Cuban soil to deter any future American invasion attempt. Construction of the missile sites began late in the summer of 1962. JFK, made aware by the CIA of a general Soviet arms buildup on Cuba, issued a public warning on September 4 that America would not tolerate the introduction of Soviet offensive weapons onto the island. On September 11, Moscow, blatantly lying, assured the worried White House all weapons sent to Castro were purely defensive in nature, stating that it had no need for nuclear missiles to be transferred to any country outside of the Soviet Union. However, on October 14, the U-2 spy planes sighted the missile installations near San Cristobal in western Cuba.

The Soviet missiles had a range of 1,200 miles, able to strike most of the US mainland on a moment's notice. Far more important, however, was the political threat the missiles posed. JFK had campaigned for the presidency as a tough Cold Warrior, factually incorrectly but politically effectively castigating his Republican presidential opponent, Vice President Richard Nixon, as presiding over a missile gap favoring the Soviets.

Yet Kennedy's standing had taken a beating early in his term, along with general American credibility. Now, he had irrefutable evidence that he had been lied to. Worse, despite his explicit warnings of US action should Khrushchev arm Castro with offensive nuclear weapons, the Soviets had done so anyway.

As Arthur M. Schlesinger, Jr., a Kennedy aide as well as serving as his court historian, made clear, "American acquiescence in their deployment, Kennedy understood, would demonstrate the Soviet ability to act with impunity in the very heart of the American zone of vital interest. Soviet missiles in Cuba might not upset the strategic balance, but they would certainly upset the political balance and have a profoundly destabilizing effect on the world power equilibrium."[3]

Schlesinger, as an avowed Wilsonian, is if anything underselling the geostrategic blow such an outcome would have inflicted on the United States. For if the Soviets were allowed to place missiles in Cuba, nothing less than the Monroe Doctrine itself would lie in tatters, along with the notion of American global leadership. What followed were thirteen days of crisis (October 16–28), where the world stood on the knife's edge of nuclear war.

JFK meets Dr. Strangelove

Between October 16 and 22, 1962, unbeknownst to the rest of the world, the ExComm debated in secret how to respond to the massively destabilizing Soviet threat. At first, there simply seemed no way around armed confrontation. As Bobby Kennedy later recounted, the president "was convinced from the beginning that he would have to do something."[4] All the Joint Chiefs of Staff, to a man, favored a US air strike to destroy the missiles, followed by a ground invasion of Cuba, ridding America of Castro's menace once and for all.

For the Chiefs, unlike for JFK, America's core national interests were not primarily about avoiding war (nuclear or otherwise), or even really about removing the missiles. Instead, Castro's revolutionary government was seen as the root of all evil. Having failed to dislodge it during the Bay of Pigs, the missile crisis was viewed as an opportunity to do the job right, come what may.

The living embodiment of the military's disastrously wrongheaded stance was Air Force chief of staff General Curtis LeMay. Soon to be caricatured in Stanley Kubrick's peerless satire of the lunacies of the nuclear stand-off, *Dr. Strangelove*, as both Sterling Hayden's General Jack D. Ripper and George C. Scott's General Buck Turgidson, LeMay was unrelentingly for war over Cuba, whatever the price.

Born November 15, 1906, LeMay had been in charge of implementing America's strategic bombing campaign in the Pacific during World War II. Belligerent, relentless, and able, LeMay had planned and executed the fire-bombing strategy directed against Japanese cities, using napalm at low altitudes to inflict horrendous damage on the enemy, particularly in terms of civilian casualties.

The program had reached its hideous apogee with the fire-bombing of Tokyo on the night of March 9–10, 1945, which killed 100,000 civilians and left fully 1 million homeless, figures slightly greater than the damage caused by the nuclear bomb unleashed at Hiroshima. LeMay drily noted that if the Allies lost the war, he would surely be tried and hanged as a war criminal.

After the war, LeMay had been placed in charge of the successful 1948 Berlin airlift, a significant American success in the nascent Cold War, with US aircraft dropping massive amounts of supplies to keep a blockaded West Berlin going. Convinced the Kennedy brothers were weaklings, likely to sell out American interests to the Soviets, LeMay was grimly determined to push the young president toward open conflict over Cuba, in order to remove Castro at all costs.

For the military, "the missiles provided the *occasion* to deal with the issue for which they were prepared; ridding the Western Hemisphere of Castro's Communism."[5] LeMay and the Joint Chiefs of Staff fundamentally disagreed with Kennedy on what core national security interests were at stake over the missile crisis. As historian Martin Sherwin put it, "The Chiefs' objective was to be in the best position to fight a war, while the president's aim was to select the strategy that was least likely to start a war."[6]

Pressuring the president, LeMay told Kennedy that the Russians would do nothing in the face of a US invasion of Cuba, as they simply could not start a nuclear war. Appalled at this level of nuclear brinksmanship, JFK demurred, saying, "They can't let us … take out their missiles, kill a lot of Russians and not do anything."[7]

Fortunately for the world, the Bay of Pigs disaster had taught the by-nature skeptical Kennedy to distrust the national security establishment—the foreign policy blob of its day. As JFK was to later tell Schlesinger, "The military are mad. They wanted to do this [invade]. It's lucky for us we have [Secretary of Defense Robert] McNamara over there."[8] As Kennedy sardonically told his senior aide Dave Powers, "These brass hats have one great advantage in their favor. If we listen to them and do what they want us to do, none of us will be alive later to tell them that they were wrong."[9]

Yet Kennedy, initially almost entirely isolated in the ExComm, continued to look for another way. Hewing to his laser-like focus on core American national interests driving his foreign policy, JFK knew that military action against Khrushchev and Castro would start the ball rolling toward nuclear midnight. As historians Richard Neustadt and

Graham Allison recount, outside the ExComm conference room at the State Department there was a sign: "In the nuclear age, superpowers make war like porcupines make love—carefully."[10]

Aware of the calamitous stakes involved, Kennedy instead looked—despite the fierce resistance of LeMay, the Chiefs, and congressional hard-liners—for a diplomatic approach that would leave all his options open.

In classical realist fashion, Kennedy instinctively and immediately tried to game out Khrushchev's motivations. At one ExComm meeting, the president tried to fathom his counterpart's motivations: "We ought to think of why the Russians did this."[11] Kennedy was determined to give Khrushchev as much political space to back down as possible, in line with his two core foreign-policy objectives of getting the missiles out and avoiding war. As the president told his brother, "I am not going to push the Russians an inch beyond what is necessary."[12]

Summing up, RFK was to say, "The final lesson of the Cuban missile crisis is the importance of placing ourselves in the other country's shoes. During the crisis, President Kennedy spent more time trying to determine the effect of a particular course of action on Khrushchev or the Russians than on any other phase of what he was doing. What guided all his deliberations was an effort not to disgrace Khrushchev, not to humiliate the Soviet Union, not to have them feel they would have to escalate their response."[13] Above all, JFK did not want to push the Soviets into choosing between a disgraceful diplomatic defeat and nuclear war.

It was imperative that Kennedy give Khrushchev some breathing room, for as we now know the Soviet leader was at the very same time having problems with hard-liners of his own. As Khrushchev later recounted to the *Saturday Review*'s Norman Cousins (an unofficial emissary between the Soviet leader and the president), when he asked the Soviet military whether keeping the missiles in Cuba wouldn't bring about nuclear war, they looked at him "as though I were out of my mind or, what was worse, a traitor. So, I said to myself, 'To hell with these maniacs.'"[14]

As was true with Khrushchev, Kennedy was all too aware that the situation could quickly and disastrously get out of hand. He had been much impressed by Barbara Tuchman's *The Guns of August*, a startling account of how the nations of Europe had stumbled into the charnel house of World War I, a conflict almost none of them had wanted. Determined to avoid absent-mindedly letting loose the dogs of war, JFK "took the greatest care to keep the armed forces on the tightest leash, much to their ill-concealed irritation."[15]

Kennedy did not know then, as we do now, that Soviet tactical nukes were lying in wait in Cuba, which may well have been the surprise triggering any American invasion into nuclear war. But he sensed, and he feared, as in August 1914, the awful unpredictability of unforeseen events driving the world over the abyss. As the president said at the time, "If we attack the missiles or invade Cuba it gives them [the Soviets] a clear line to take [West] Berlin."[16]

The deadly hair-trigger nature of war would then take its horrible course. If the Americans invaded Cuba, the Soviets would invade Berlin. If the Soviets invaded Berlin, America—per the NATO treaty—would come to its German ally's defense. General war would lie at the end of this lethal equation. This dreadful calculation drove Kennedy to look for another way out of the crisis, short of the invasion of Cuba which could well trigger the apocalypse.

Kennedy finds a way: the quarantine

On October 21, 1962, the ExComm met again to consider two policy options: an air strike against the Cuban missile bases, or a naval block-ade. The greatest problem of the latter was that it did nothing to remove the missiles already on Cuba, and the Russians might launch a break-neck program to try to complete the missile installations already there, even as they complied with the too-late quarantine (which is precisely what happened).

However, the positives of following such a policy entirely were greater than the negatives. It allowed Kennedy the flexibility to still increase the pressure on the Soviets, without immediately plunging the world into war. At the same time, Kennedy's twin overriding primary American interests—to get all the missiles out of Cuba and to avoid nuclear confla-gration—might yet be achieved.

Brainy Secretary of Defense Robert McNamara, who had come up with the quarantine policy suggestion, became its strongest proponent. He argued it amounted to forceful, if limited, pressure on the Soviets—a dramatic gesture which still left the administration in control of events.

The ExComm was split down the middle, with many hard-liners (including but not limited to the Joint Chiefs of Staff) continuing to call for an immediate air strike. However, in terms of bureaucratic politics, the quarantine was supported by the administration's heavy hitters, those most respected and closest to the president himself. The blockade policy was supported by McNamara, Bobby Kennedy, and Ted Sorensen, "a powerful coalition of advisers in whom the President had the greatest confidence, and with whom he was personally most compatible."[17]

In the dramatic phrasing of Robert Kennedy, "It was now up to one single man."[18] Finally, on October 22, Kennedy decided on a naval quarantine of Cuba. The use of the term "quarantine" was to distinguish American naval actions from that of a "blockade," which was technically an act of war. This rhetorical toning-down of Washington's policy enabled the US to gain the unanimous diplomatic support of the Organization of American States (OAS)—a regional multilateral organization—for the action. The Soviets and Cubans now faced the united diplomatic resolve of the whole of the Western Hemisphere.

At the same time, in a private letter to Khrushchev explaining his actions, Kennedy declared that the US would not permit any further offensive weapons to be delivered to Cuba, while demanding that the USSR dismantle the missile bases already under construction and return all offensive nuclear missiles to Russia. That evening, JFK went on television, informing the public of the crisis and his policy for dealing with it in enforcing the quarantine.

We know now that Khrushchev, echoing Kennedy's cautious moves to avoid the unthinkable, ordered the immediate turning back of all Soviet ships carrying further missiles to Cuba. Sure enough, by October 25, all Soviet ships carrying offensive weapons had stopped short of the US naval quarantine line. However, at the same time, he was as yet unprepared to relinquish the missiles already ensconced on the island. The Kennedy administration had scored a tactical victory, but the crisis was far from over.

* * *

Meanwhile, further U-2 flights over Cuba showed that the missile sites were nearly operational. On October 25, Kennedy told his advisers that it appeared that only a US attack on Cuba would lead to the removal of the missiles, but that he wanted to give the diplomatic track more time in the hopes that cooler heads would prevail.

It was Khrushchev who provided Kennedy his long-sought opening. ABC news reporter John Scali alerted the White House that he had been approached by Alexander Feklisov, the Soviet KGB station chief in Washington and a personal friend of the Soviet premier, suggesting an agreement could be reached if the US would accept publicly promising not to invade Cuba in return for Soviet missiles being removed from the island.

Supporting this back-channel feeler, the Soviet leader sent the president a long, emotional personal letter on the evening of October 26.

While laying out the specter of coming nuclear holocaust, it also again proposed this diplomatic solution as a way out. As he put it, if there was no intention to doom the world to the catastrophe of nuclear war, "let us take measures to untie that knot."[19] But even before the beleaguered Kennedy team could breathe a sigh of relief, "Black Saturday," October 27, 1962, the single most dangerous day in the history of the world, had dawned.

Surviving Black Saturday

It was a day when every possible event seemed to conspire to push the world over the brink into nuclear cataclysm. Taken on their own, each of these events was ominous. Put together, they seemed to leave JFK no option but to launch the military invasion that he feared would be the start of World War III.

First, early in the morning, the White House received another letter from Khrushchev. Very different in tone from his anguished missive of the previous night, this letter—which the CIA rightly assessed as having been written by the collective Soviet Politburo leadership rather than Khrushchev alone—was more demanding, aggressive, and unyielding. It stressed that any proposed deal must also include the removal of American Jupiter nuclear missiles pointed at the Kremlin from Turkey. This toughening of Soviet terms enraged the hard-liners around JFK, who contended that the Russians were reneging on the earlier deal, opening a diplomatic bazaar, asking for an endless series of concessions from a pliant America.

Even here, JFK alone saw a way out. Practically, the deterrent function of the Jupiter missiles was negligible, soon taken over more effectively by Polaris nuclear missiles that could be launched from submarines. However, Kennedy rightly conceded the hard-liners' point that to make the removal of the missiles in Turkey a quid pro quo for the Soviets dismantling the missiles in Cuba, it would seem to reward their aggressive behavior. Only by secretly agreeing to remove the missiles at a later date could a deal be salvaged. But Kennedy must be lauded for having the diplomatic imagination to see the toughening Soviet line not as an insuperable problem, and recognizing that there was still light at the end of the tunnel.

But even as the president was threading the diplomatic needle, a series of random, unrelated events pushed the world perilously close to nuclear war. First, a U-2 spy plane, navigating off the wrong star, strayed into Soviet airspace over Siberia and was chased out of Russian territory by Soviet fighter planes after ninety hair-raising minutes. This mistaken act obviously looked aggressive to a Russia aware that General LeMay's Strategic Air Command was on a nuclear hair-trigger.

Second, and historically we now know most ominously, *B-59*, a Soviet submarine in the Atlantic, was forced to the surface by depth charges from USS *Beale*. Unbeknownst to the Americans, *B-59* had torpedoes aboard armed with fifteen-kiloton nuclear warheads. Command for when to fire the warheads normally devolved to the captain of the sub and the political commissar aboard, who looked after the interests of the Communist Party. *B-59* had been beyond radio contact, deep under the sea in an effort to evade American detection. It had no communication with Moscow for several days and was unaware of the quarantine. The submarine surfaced not knowing whether the Soviet Union was at war or peace.

The commander of *B-59*, Captain Valentin Savitsky, insisted that the depth charges were a sign that war had broken out. However, the commander of the entire submarine flotilla, Vasily Arkhipov, was also billeted aboard. Crucially, he too had a say as to when and whether the sub's nuclear torpedoes could be launched. While Savitsky and the commissar were determined to launch their warheads, Arkhipov—to his everlasting credit—would not be budged, even as an argument broke out between the three as to what to do.

Eventually Arkhipov persuaded a harassed Savitsky to surface and await orders from Moscow, which told him to head back to the Soviet Union. While Arkhipov's act of heroism certainly prevented World War III from breaking out, it also underlined that both Khrushchev and Kennedy were losing control of events, and perilously quickly.

Third, tragically an American U-2 spy plane was shot down over Cuba. Major Rudolf Anderson's plane was struck by a surface-to-air missile guarding one of the nuclear installations. In terms of the military's rules of engagement, JFK had previously agreed that if an American pilot was fired upon (let alone killed), air strikes on the offending anti-aircraft site would be the minimum US response, followed by the American invasion of Cuba.

Bravely, and determined not to be boxed in by the military, Kennedy went back on his earlier decision, as he did not think the attack had been ordered by the Soviet Union.* He agreed to initiate strikes, but only if another attack was made and a pattern of aggression was established. At just this inopportune moment, the CIA confirmed that all the missiles on the ground in Cuba were now operational. The clock was ticking.

Something had to be done, or Barbara Tuchman's *Guns of August* scenario was soon to overwhelm both leaders, as unforeseen events would lead to a deadly logic of their own. Up against the wall, JFK sent his closest adviser, brother Bobby, to meet with Soviet ambassador Anatoly Dobrynin in the attorney general's office at 7:45 p.m. on Black Saturday. It was now or never for a deal. Focusing entirely on America's primary interests—to get the missiles out while avoiding nuclear war—RFK outlined his brother's plan to the ambassador.

In an effort to make the gravity of the situation clear, Bobby told Dobrynin that the US was aware that work was almost complete on the

---

* About this point, JFK was historically correct, as later it emerged that the missile was fired by Cuban troops on the ground.

missile bases in Cuba. RFK went on to say that Major Anderson had been killed that day. Focusing on Khrushchev's first, more emollient letter, the attorney general went on to accept the soviet premier's terms for removing the missiles from Cuba under UN supervision in exchange for an American pledge not to invade.

However, time was of the essence. The US would need a commitment by the very next day (October 28) that the missiles would be removed. Bluntly, Bobby told the ambassador that "he [Dobrynin] should understand that if they [the Soviets] did not remove the missiles, we [the United States] would remove them."[20] Further, in a secret protocol, the administration accepted the terms of the second letter—that the US would withdraw the obsolete Jupiter missiles from Turkey several months later—but on the condition that the deal would be null and void should the Soviets disclose its existence.* Also distrusting his hard-liners, Khrushchev approved JFK's terms without again consulting the Politburo, in a October 28 broadcast on Radio Moscow.

As I noted in another book, "On its surface, these terms were not unduly unfavorable for the Soviet Union."[21] The USSR's ally Fidel Castro—perpetual thorn in the side of the United States—had just been granted his continuing existence, which had been the point of installing the missiles in the first place. Further, there was strategic reciprocity in the deal, as the missiles which sat all-too-close to the United States in Cuba had been removed in return for the removal of missiles sitting all-too-close to the Soviet Union in Turkey.

While all this is true, there is also little doubt that the Cuban Missile Crisis was a public relations disaster for the USSR, just as it was a triumph for Jack Kennedy. According to Ambassador Dobrynin, "the top Soviet leadership took the Cuban outcome as 'a blow to its prestige bordering on

---

* The Khrushchev regime kept the secret and the Jupiter missiles were removed in April 1963.

humiliation.'"[22] Premier Khrushchev, as a direct result of the crisis, was removed by a Soviet coup led by Leonid Brezhnev in October 1964.

Pensioned off by the plotters, Khrushchev was allotted an apartment and even a small dacha in the country. Nevertheless, he fell into a deep depression over his forced retirement, becoming a Soviet "non-person." Dying of a heart attack on September 11, 1971, Khrushchev was even denied the recognition of a state funeral by his enemies.

Tragedy after saving the world

As for General LeMay, JFK's wrongheaded nemesis throughout the Cuban Missile Crisis, his life ended up going in about the direction one would have guessed. Madly suggesting that Cuba should be invaded anyway after the crisis had reached its peaceful conclusion, LeMay was finally eased out of the Pentagon by McNamara in February 1965.

Running for vice president as a third-party candidate with the populist segregationist George Wallace in 1968, LeMay was viewed as too much of a wild card by the canny southern leader, being seen as a liability. He was quickly sidelined in the campaign. Nevertheless, the Wallace-LeMay ticket won 13.5 percent of the popular vote that fateful year, taking five southern states and 46 electoral votes, a highly impressive showing for such an insurgent campaign. But LeMay was done in American politics. He died October 1, 1990, a largely forgotten figure.

As for Kennedy, as the years have gone on since the missile crisis, his crowning achievement has been somewhat obscured, hidden in the mist of his legend. Good-looking, charming, eloquent, JFK was a matinee-idol president—the most glamorous chief executive the country has ever had. Sadly, his evident style has come to obscure the substance of his achievement in the Cuban Missile Crisis.

For as the historical record recounts, had someone else been president, had almost anyone else been president, it is highly likely that there would have been another, far more disastrous, outcome to the crisis. Kennedy was a believer in the "great man" theory of history—that people, and not only large global forces, control the world's destiny. In October 1962, with his own idiosyncratic genius, he was to prove the validity of all that he believed.

Kennedy's magic compass, his realist fixation on the notion that only primary national interests should drive US foreign policy, saw him through the most dangerous moment the world has ever endured. It allowed the president to avoid all the noise emanating from the crisis and to instead focus only on the essential. For JFK, that meant, above all else, getting the Soviet missiles out of Cuba without triggering a nuclear war. Everything else was negotiable, and all tactics that furthered these primary interests were to be entertained. By his own primary-interest yardstick, JFK was successful, somehow achieving this seemingly impossible feat.

Since Kennedy's time, the noise, if anything, has grown in US foreign policy decision-making circles. There are fully hundreds of articles my political risk staff and I can choose to read on any given day, most of them trivial, either in terms of what they have to say or in their failure to focus on regions and countries which are primary American interests.

Wilsonians, in particular, have confronted this confusing reality by making endless laundry lists as to what America should do in the world, being completists who catalog without discrimination every possible US foreign policy initiative without ever asking which US interests are paramount, which are important, and which are entirely peripheral, merely being on a good day what the US might like to happen. Intellectually, it is a way around making choices, for if everything is as important as the Wilsonian-dominated US foreign policy establishment seems to think it is in its stubborn refusal to prioritize, then in reality nothing is important.

For example, for all the noise, Ukraine is a sideshow in terms of primary American interests, not having anywhere near the geostrategic importance the Biden administration's blank check has implicitly given it. On the other hand, the Indo-Pacific, where much of the world's future economic growth is located as well as much of the world's future political risk, meets the "Kennedy test" as to what a primary American national interest presently looks like.

To try to do everything in foreign policy is to do everything poorly, for even a country as rich and powerful as the United States has limits. Worse, the no-limits approach leads directly to imperial overstretch, failure, and decline for the great power incapable of making strategic choices based on articulating primary national interests.

Kennedy took the realist intellectual road less traveled, focusing only on primary US foreign policy interests and letting go of worrying about all the rest. Such an approach forced him to make choices, to prioritize getting the missiles out of Cuba in order to restore the world's geostrategic equilibrium while at the same time avoiding the calamity of nuclear war.

While the Cuban Missile Crisis raged, China invaded India, a not-insignificant strategic event even in faraway 1962. When informed of this by Bobby, Jack Kennedy stuck to his realist guns, saying he could only deal with one crisis at a time. This laser-like focus on the essential— on primary American national interests—was the secret to Kennedy's success in 1962. In our own era of endless international trivia, it is even more important in managing our cacophonous world.

* * *

Khrushchev was not alone in having the fates turn against him after the missiles of October. Jack Kennedy, given the tragic deaths of his older brother and favorite sister, plus his perennial debilitating health problems,[23] had always held a tragic view of life, a sense that one's time on earth was fleeting. As Bobby later recounted, just after the crisis came to an end the president turned toward him and sardonically noted, "As I was leaving, he said, making reference to Abraham Lincoln, 'This is the night I should go to the theater.' I said, 'If you go, I want to go with you.'"[24] Jack would be killed just one year later, and then Bobby in 1968. But it is not too much to say that the Kennedy brothers saved the world.

~ 8 ~

DEALING WITH THE DEVIL

*Nixon's pivot to China is the game
changer in the Cold War*

Realism masters the Cold War

By the time Richard Milhous Nixon finally made it to the White House in January 1969, the Cold War had been dragging on for an unedifying two decades, with no end in sight. Worse, the United States, if anything, seemed to be falling behind its Soviet competitors. The previous year, 1968, had been just awful for the country with the assassinations of Martin Luther King Jr. and Robert Kennedy, fraught race relations triggering mass inner-city violence, and pitched battles fought on the streets of Chicago between police and the youthful (and increasingly radicalized) Vietnam protestors at the Democratic National Convention. It seemed as if America itself was coming apart at the seams.

Nixon, one of the most able (and among the strangest) men ever to assume the presidency, was to dramatically turn the tables on this narrative of domestic decline and international stasis. Most American presidents come to power with no actual fixed intellectual program regarding foreign policy. The events they encounter and their responses to them flesh out their thinking after the fact.

This was very much not the case with the Nixon presidency. With world-class foreign policy intellectual Henry Kissinger serving as his national security advisor and chief foreign policy partner, Nixon came to the Oval Office with a set of fixed realist principles that he was determined to implement across the globe. The duo's undeniable success is first and foremost due to this critical fact; that they first thought through how the world actually worked, and then devised foreign policy initiatives to fit their realist point of view, rather than merely being tossed about by the tide of history.

Nixon and Kissinger observed that America was simply not winning the long-standing Cold War contest with the Soviet Union. As they clearly saw this to be the case, realism impelled them to do the next obvious thing: change the rules of a game that wasn't going well for the country. In his incredibly bold opening to China, Nixon was to do just this, dealing with the devil that was Mao's incredibly bloody regime, and in doing so mastering the Cold War itself.

The realist rationale for the China pivot

At the opening of Nixon's term, the idea that the American president would visit the People's Republic of China (PRC) was about as likely as him going to the moon. Since Communist victory in the Chinese Civil War in 1949, for twenty-two years there had been no commercial or diplomatic ties between the world's foremost superpower and the most populous country on earth. The US continued to recognize the Chinese Nationalist Kuomintang government of Chiang Kai-shek—which had fled the Chinese mainland for the island of Taiwan following defeat in the civil war—as the sole government of China, whatever the reality.

The reasons for this strategic estrangement were legion. At the time, almost every American policy-maker (wrongly) saw the communist bloc—headed by the USSR but with China as an emerging, if still junior, partner—as monolithic "international communism," marching in lockstep to defeat the western, capitalist forces headed by the United States. If anything, with the death of Stalin in 1953, it was Mao's regime which was viewed as the more ideologically stridently anti-American of the two, having actually gone to war with the United States in Korea, 1950–3.

Even if the communist bloc was breaking up (as was actually the case in the 1960s), how could the US treat with a blood-soaked regime that would come to kill an incomprehensible 40–80 million of its own people through starvation, persecution, prison labor, and mass executions?[1] Even given the trinity of twentieth-century evil—Hitler, Stalin, and Mao—the Chairman was surely the Ted Bundy of international relations. How could Nixon work with such a monster?

The simple answer was that, in doing so, he mightily furthered America's primary interests. Sensing that vague reports of a fundamental split between the USSR and China were real, Nixon almost immediately moved to exploit the schism. First, there was the diplomatic prize of China itself. As Nixon had written in "Asia After Vietnam," a *Foreign Affairs* article in 1967, "Taking the long view, we simply cannot afford to leave China forever outside the family of nations."[2] It was simply too big, too populous, had too much economic potential, and was too strategically important to remain eternally an international pariah.

Second, and this was Nixon's initial focus for the pivot, the president felt improved ties with Beijing (or Peking, as it was called then) could be a cudgel used to pressure the Soviets into reaching an arms control deal over nuclear weapons, and even lead to a more general superpower détente. Washington would gain a new heavyweight partner to counter Moscow, which would put the Soviets on the defensive. More specifically, it was (wrongly) hoped that in the new strategic environment, Moscow might be forced to lessen its support for an increasingly victorious North Vietnam.

Third, Kissinger, even going beyond this, came to see the China pivot as changing the very global balance of power—the world's polarity—itself. "Instead of using improved relations with Beijing primarily as a bludgeon to threaten Moscow [as Nixon stressed], he envisioned a triangular set of relations that could create a more stable world balance. 'We moved toward China ... to shape a global equilibrium.'"[3]

While within this tripolar system—the first significant power change at the global geostrategic level since the Cold War had begun a quarter century before—the US was still individually by far the most powerful player. However, the key to America's ultimate advantage would lie in the fact that it was the fulcrum of this new global power reality. The United States was central in that both other great powers would come to have better ties with America than either had with each other. Fearing isolation, both would move toward the US at the same time.

So, the pivot to China, invaluable on its own terms, amounted to much more. It came to define a new power reality at the global level, one that greatly favored a formerly beleaguered America. As Kissinger later put it, "To have the two Communist powers competing for good relations with us could only benefit the cause of peace. It was the essence of the triangular strategy."[4] If that meant treating with the devil that was Mao, then so be it, to secure American primacy in a very dangerous world.

Here Nixon's specific biography came to his rescue as the ultimate Cold Warrior. Throughout the whole of his political career, since his days as a congressman on the House Un-American Activities Committee (HUAC), exposing communist influence in the State Department, Nixon had made his name as an avowed anti-communist. Given his strident, rightist, hawkish credentials, it was politically very hard to argue that the president made it a practice to be "soft on communism."

In fact, the White House's political strategy over the China pivot proved so successful that it spawned an idiom. "Only Nixon could go to China" came to mean in English that a person's past reputation would actually shield them from making seemingly contradictory moves in life, defying conventional wisdom. As the historian Timothy Naftali wisely notes, given the lock-step ideological anti-communism governing the American elite at the time, "I believe the argument that only Richard Nixon could have done this in American politics."[5]

For the Chinese, the dramatic diplomatic about-face made realist sense as well. Beyond their huge ideological and values gulf, specific practical realist interests—above all, a common desire to resist the spread of Soviet influence—gravitationally pushed these very odd allies decisively together, as interests almost always ultimately determine foreign policy decision-making. For monolithic communism was a thing of the past.

The Sino-Soviet split emerged over Soviet premier Nikita Khrushchev's more moderate leadership after the death of Stalin in March 1953, and his electrifying denunciation of the excesses of the Soviet dictator in 1956. Mao, who like Stalin ran a personality-driven dictatorship, felt threatened by Khrushchev's charges. Pushing the twin reformist policies of de-Stalinization and peaceful coexistence with the west, Khrushchev was almost immediately met by very public and embarrassing resistance from Mao's regime over both points.

Beyond these broad differences, a divergence over a number of specific policy areas quickly emerged. The Soviets reneged on a commitment to provide China with a prototype nuclear bomb in 1957. Despite the Great Chinese Famine of 1959–61—when Mao's economic illiteracy with the Great Leap Forward modernization program led directly to the deaths of 15–55 million[6]—Moscow insisted on receiving grain export shipments already agreed upon. Khrushchev became Mao's convenient scapegoat in place of his obvious culpability for this calamity.[7]

Likewise, Beijing resented the USSR's increased ties to India, even as China engaged in a sporadic border war with New Delhi. For his part, the Soviet premier was horrified at the flippant way the Chairman often referred to nuclear war. Ideologically poles apart, by 1961 the PRC formally demonized Soviet communism as the work of "revisionist traitors."

But beneath these very real differences in ideas, the schism was also about practical power—the "Batman problem" as to who was going to lead the communist world, and who was destined to merely play the part of sidekick (Robin). When Khrushchev criticized seemingly unimportant

Albania's Enver Hoxha for running the place like a Stalinist prison, Mao leapt to his fellow communist dictator's defense.

For what Moscow and Peking were vying for was nothing less than the global leadership of communism. Finally, in late 1962, the PRC broke off relations with the Soviet Union, for the nonsensical reason (but it did look good at the time to other communists around the world) that the Soviet premier had not gone to nuclear war with the Kennedy brothers over the Cuban Missile Crisis.

Eventually, the rivalry led to outright blows. Beginning in March 1969 and lasting for seven months, an undeclared Sino-Soviet border war raged along the Ussuri River demarcating the boundary between the two countries. This, above all, convinced China that the Soviet Union was the bigger strategic threat than America. As such, it needed protection from the stronger Soviets. The Nixon administration was the logical place for Mao to turn.

A secret plan bears fruit

For all of Kissinger's later brilliant contributions, at the beginning the China pivot was entirely Richard Nixon's idea. Only one week into his term of office, the president called his national security advisor, telling him he wanted to open relations with the PRC. A skeptical Kissinger relayed Nixon's desire to H.R. Haldeman, Nixon's ferocious chief of staff, saying such a pipedream would never come to pass. But, then again, Richard Nixon was used to being underestimated.

Nixon was a curious, and very odd, mix of personal contradictions. The thirty-seventh president was born January 9, 1913, on his family's small lemon ranch in Yorba Linda, California. His childhood was marred by hardships, ranging from the premature deaths of two of his brothers to his Quaker family's economic struggles. In 1922, the family moved to Whittier, California, where Frank Nixon opened a small grocery store and gas station and scratched to make a living. Although he managed to gain entrance to Harvard with a scholarship (his intellectual abilities were always plain to see), young Dick stayed home at Whittier College to be near to his parents as they cared for his terminally ill eldest brother, Harold.

Along with lingering, strange resentments that festered all his life about the difficult start he had endured (as opposed to say, his rival Jack Kennedy), Nixon's iron will soon became apparent. Graduating with highest academic honors from Whittier, he was accepted at the prestigious Duke University School of Law, where he finished third in his class. However, despite this first-rate academic pedigree, Nixon—bereft of any contacts to open doors for him—could not find a legal position in New York. Disappointed, and a little embittered, he returned to California.

Nixon served honorably as an officer in the navy in the Solomon Islands during World War II before heading home and almost immediately becoming immersed in California politics. His rise as a hawkish Republican Cold Warrior saw him enter the House of Representatives in 1947, where he quickly made a name for himself on the HUAC, investigating Alger Hiss, a leading diplomat from the days of FDR, who was accused of being a Soviet spy. After an epic personal confrontation between the two men, Hiss was eventually convicted of perjury, just as Nixon's national reputation as a staunch anti-communist was made. Rising quickly, he was decisively elected to the Senate in 1950, but he was not to stay there for long.

For in 1952, Eisenhower, almost sure to win the presidency, chose Nixon to be his running mate. While he knew little of the young senator at the time (and never particularly liked or trusted Nixon, despite the fact that the vice president's daughter Julie would come to marry Eisenhower's grandson David), Nixon had complementary qualities that suited the ticket. He was young, came from the right wing of the party, was a vigorous campaigner never afraid to get into the mud with his opponents, and came from California, a vital electoral asset, then as now.

After eight years serving as vice president, Nixon went into the election of 1960 the obvious successor to Eisenhower within the GOP and the favorite in the presidential contest with the untested John F. Kennedy. However, it was in 1960 that JFK's matinee-idol charisma came to the fore, a reality which bedeviled the dour Nixon, even as he was uneasily aware of its power. In the end, in one of the closest election results ever, Kennedy beat Nixon by just .2 percent of the popular vote, or a paltry 112,000 votes—the difference amounting to the number of people in a medium-sized town in a continent full of them.

Despite real voting irregularities in Texas (spearheaded by Lyndon Johnson's cronies) and Chicago (where the Democratic mayor, Richard J. Daley, ruled the roost), Nixon refused to contest the 1960 result, sparing the country the ordeal of a recount. While he did the right and honorable thing, Nixon never forgot his defeat at the hands of Kennedy, the establishment darling, who seemed to exemplify all the grace and charm that Nixon so painfully, for all his many gifts, lacked. His anger at his enemies and the world grew.

Staging a remarkable comeback, Nixon finally vaulted into power in 1968, defeating Vice President Hubert Humphrey in another agonizingly close result, ending up winning the popular vote by less than one percentage point, or 500,000 votes.* Nixon brought both his great strengths and his gaping flaws to the presidency. Secretive, awkward, driven, uneasy, iron-willed, highly intelligent, sly, solitary, paranoid, creative, and resentful, "Nixon was a great statesman on the world stage as well as a shabby practitioner of electoral politics in the domestic arena."[8]

---

* He won the electoral college more comfortably, with 301 electors to Humphrey's 191.

This very strange man was to have one of the most controversial of presidencies, scaling almost unimagined heights and yet committing political suicide through a series of avoidable, self-inflicted wounds that robbed him of the greatness that was his for the taking.

However, all that was in the future. The unfolding diplomatic drama that was the pivot to China played to the president's character, as it was epitomized by boldness, an expert intellectual realist grasp of geostrategy, secrecy, and elaborate deception. As the overtures to China went on, not even the vice president or the Secretary of State was aware of what was going on. For the American side, Nixon and the able Kissinger managed the initiative almost entirely alone.

The president chose to use the Pakistani government of General Yahya Khan as a back-door conduit, as Islamabad was uniquely friendly with both Washington and Beijing. As far back as Nixon's August 1969 trip around the world, he had personally asked Khan to convey to Mao's regime that the White House was willing to start a new relationship with the PRC.

In October 1970, Nixon followed up, as Khan was given a letter for Chinese premier Zhou Enlai, proposing sending an American emissary to China to discuss the possibility of a presidential visit, which the Pakistani president relayed a week later. For the Pakistani side, only its president and foreign minister knew what was going on, as secrecy was vital if the whole initiative were to have a ghost of a chance.

A host of outside forces would dearly have loved to strangle the groundbreaking foreign policy gambit at birth. From Nixon's point of view, subterfuge preserved the great drama of the occasion, and circumvented the establishment State Department bureaucracy from killing it, all while avoiding paralyzing public and congressional debate derailing the pivot. Finally, Nixon headed off conservatives in his own party, avowed anti-communists like himself, who would have scuttled the whole effort. As Nixon bluntly said, "Simply put, we could never have done it if we had not kept it secret."[9]

Finally, on April 21, 1971, after waiting more than six months, China sent its favorable reply. Mao conditionally was inviting Nixon to China, but only after an emissary (the irrepressible Kissinger was suggested by name) visited to negotiate the details. As Kissinger grandly put to Nixon, "This is the most important communication that has come to an American president since the end of World War II."[10]

This was all to be done in secret. The elaborate deception began on July 1, 1971, with Kissinger heading off on a "fact-finding tour" of Asia. Once he reached Pakistan, Kissinger feigned illness, requiring him to rest at a hill station in the Himalayas, far removed from Islamabad. There, the Pakistani foreign minister personally drove Kissinger to an airfield and he was whisked off to China.

In his haste, Kissinger had forgotten to bring along any spare shirts for his diplomatic mission, being forced to borrow much larger spares from one of his aides. When the pictures of his meetings in China were eventually released, the vain national security advisor looked delighted, though also as if he was drowning in his clothes. Worse, as he later puckishly recounted, the shirts were made in Taiwan.

Kissinger finally landed in Beijing on July 9, 1971. This able practitioner of realism was under the gun, having only forty-eight hours to nail down the terms for the coming visit. For the Chinese side, Mao had deputized his indispensable ally, Zhou Enlai, to work out the deal with Kissinger. Zhou was cultured and educated where Mao was crude and blunt, and stoic while Mao was paranoid. He was also urbane, gaunt, graceful, worldly, and utterly loyal to Mao to the point of subservience.

The Chinese premier made a great impression on Nixon's man. Kissinger noted Zhou's expressive face, intense, piercing eyes, and the self-confidence which had enabled him to survive every one of Mao's purges (though two of his adopted children were tortured and murdered by Red Guards in 1966 during the lunacy of Mao's Cultural Revolution).

Ultimately, he would serve as the Chairman's only prime minister for twenty-two storm-tossed years.

Kissinger held an exhausting seventeen hours of meetings with Zhou over these two critical days. Initially, both sides made clear that they were there because of their shared distrust of the Soviet Union. While it was apparent that the USSR drove Beijing and Washington together, it was just as apparent that their vast differences over Taiwan had the capacity (even then) to scuttle the budding alliance.

Taiwan was not the only major area of disagreement. With America coming apart over anti-war protests, Kissinger asked Zhou for help putting pressure on its communist ally in Hanoi to end the Vietnam War. Zhou bluntly replied that there was no chance of this happening and that the only solution (and here he was correct) was for US troops to leave. Kissinger and Nixon had miscalculated how steadfast the Chinese (and the Soviets, for that matter) would prove to be in support of their North Vietnamese ally.

Given these significant differences, it was by no means assured that enough would be agreed on to justify the summit taking place. To break the logjam, Zhou proposed an ingenious solution, which was readily accepted by Kissinger and laid the basis for the final Shanghai Communiqué, agreed by Nixon and the Chinese leadership during his later visit. The Chinese premier argued for a document that, while it detailed mutual Chinese and American interests in commonly resisting the Soviets throughout the world, also did not paper over their many differences, particularly regarding Taiwan. Both sides were given free rein in the document to declare unilaterally their positions over major issues where they did not agree.

As the historian Walter Isaacson shrewdly notes, "the great break-through on Taiwan was that there did not need to be a great breakthrough on Taiwan."[11] As Mao was later to say to Nixon and Kissinger during their meeting, Taiwan was not the most important matter of substance between the two great powers; it had not been resolved over the past twenty years and a resolution could wait another twenty years, even another century.*

The Shanghai Communiqué stated (to the delight of the PRC) that there was only "One China," without ever quite saying who would serve as its ultimate government, and that Taiwan was an indivisible part of such an entity. At the same time, the US reaffirmed its acute interest in a peaceful settlement of the dispute.† However, as Kissinger would darkly note, Mao made it crystal clear "that Beijing would not foreclose its option to use force over Taiwan—and indeed expected to have to use force someday."[12] And there the matter uneasily rests to this day.

The summit had been salvaged, precisely because at the time both great powers thought their interests were better served by commonly opposing Soviet adventurism, rather than fighting amongst themselves over Taiwan. To put it mildly, this is no longer the case today. However, then it was enough for Zhou, who agreed to go ahead with the earth-shattering visit.

On July 15, 1971, Nixon boldly announced on television that he would visit China the following year. "In a single stroke, the president had confounded all of his enemies: the Soviets, the North Vietnamese, the press, and the liberal Democrats."[13] Immense credit was due to the two men atop American foreign policy-making. As Roger Morris, Kissinger's former aide and frequent critic managed to admit, "Just as the China opening could not have begun and continued without Nixon's vision, it never would have been so skillfully executed without Kissinger."[14]

---

*   If only present Chinese paramount leader Xi Jinping felt this way.

†   With the Taiwan Relations Act of 1979, America was more pro-Taipei, pledging to provide Taiwan with "all necessary articles for its self-defense," without (quite) explicitly committing US troops to its defense should the PRC invade. This strategic ambiguity is where the matter now rests.

The week that changed the world

Nixon's February 21–28, 1972 visit to China was the first made by any sitting US president. While seeing Peking, Hangzhou (Mao's summer retreat), and Shanghai, the president—with television cameras in tow providing live coverage—took the American people along with him. As Isaacson observes, "For a generation, the US public and its professional ruling elite had viewed China as a fanatic revolutionary realm, a *terra incognita* of the sort that ancient cartographers used to label 'here be dragons.'"[15] For their part, with the Cultural Revolution still in full swing, the Chinese leadership had until very recently denounced Nixon personally as a bloodthirsty gangster.

Things were so uncertain and on edge that, when he landed, Nixon did not know if Chairman Mao would even deign to receive him. He needn't have worried. After ostentatiously shaking hands with Zhou—as opposed to Eisenhower's Secretary of State, John Foster Dulles, who had humiliated the premier by disdaining to do so at an international conference in the 1950s—Nixon and Kissinger were immediately whisked off to Mao's deceptively simple house within the red walls of the Imperial City in Peking.

The Chairman was there to give his official blessing to the visit, even as he deputized Zhou to handle its details and be the president's chaperone. As such, the Americans met with Mao only once, for about an hour, while they conversed with Zhou dozens of times during the trip. Unbeknownst to Nixon, at the time of the visit Mao was in poor health, having been hospitalized for several weeks until just nine days ahead of Nixon arriving in Beijing; he needed to be lifted up by aides for his momentous handshake with the president.

Self-deprecating, humorous, and simply spoken, in marked contrast to the elegant Zhou, Mao joked when he met Nixon, "I believe our old friend Chiang Kai-shek would not approve of this."[16] By bringing up

Chiang—long the ruler of Taiwan and Mao's ultimate rival—up front, the old monster put his guests at ease.

Mao later told his doctor that he had been impressed by Nixon's forthrightness during their talks, contrasting his persona favorably with both verbose western leftists and the Soviets.[17] At the same time, the Chairman distrusted the smiling Kissinger, who had ruthlessly sidelined the ineffectual Secretary of State, William Rogers, and the whole sclerotic American foreign policy apparatus from the key talks.

American television reported the visit live to a mesmerized country. Nixon was seen with his wife, Pat, on the Great Wall, at the ballet (written by Mao's venomous wife, Jiang Qing, the fanatical leader of the "Gang of Four" far-leftist faction that was perpetrating the Cultural Revolution for the Chairman), visiting the Ming tombs, exploring the Forbidden City, and at innumerable banquets.

But beneath the glittering pageantry, the substantive work of the summit went on, as the two sides toiled over the final wording of the Shanghai Communiqué, which was to govern their relations for the next generation. In the formal sessions with Zhou, the Chinese premier preferred to speak philosophically, leaving the diplomatic specifics to more junior staff, which suited Nixon to the ground, as the president also preferred talking about global strategy rather than engaging in tactical haggling.

When the dust settled and the trip came to an end, it was clear to all that a new world, based on a wholly different tripolar power structure, was in the process of being born. As Nixon grandly put it, "This was the week that changed the world."[18] While it was to take seven more years, in 1979 President Jimmy Carter and Chinese paramount leader Deng Xiaoping—Zhou's protégé, who seized power from the Gang of Four following Mao's death in 1976, and was the driver behind the country's remarkable modernization—would finally establish full diplomatic relations.

But there was absolutely no doubt that Nixon's pivot had flung the door open. As Kissinger incisively said, the trip and the China pivot "transformed the structure of international politics."[19] Even that most undemonstrative of statesman, Zhou Enlai, proclaimed that the world had shaken.[20]

Richard Nixon and Henry Kissinger, the oddest of couples, amount to one of the great double acts in American diplomatic history. Over their greatest collective geostrategic triumph, the pivot to China, there are laurels enough for both. "Nixon's original vision and persistence forced the issue; Kissinger brought the initiative to fruition and fit it into a foreign policy framework based on a triangular global balance with America at the fulcrum."[21]

Absolutely nothing would have happened without their shared realist principles that American foreign policy should be about doing good rather than feeling good. That meant moving away from the standard Wilsonian fairy tales based on simplistic notions of good and evil, and being prepared to make a deal with an undeniable devil in Mao, in order to live in a world far more conducive to basic American interests and those of its decent people.

The higher realist morality of dealing with the devil

For a while, Nixon's fabulous diplomatic winning streak continued. In May 1972, following a summit with the Soviets—clearly rattled by the China opening and far more diplomatically pliant than usual—Nixon signed the Strategic Arms Limitation Treaty, or SALT I, the first arms control agreement designed to limit the increase in nuclear weapons between the superpowers. It froze all offensive nuclear missile construction for the next five years.

Yet this record of almost unthinkable diplomatic accomplishment was to come dramatically undone by the Watergate scandal, wherein Nixon and other senior members of his administration (though not Kissinger) actively weaponized US government agencies against his enemies. In the end, for all his gifts, Nixon's paranoia got the better of him, as tragically the president brought himself down. Faced with indisputable evidence of his involvement in both the Watergate cover-up and this wider malfeasance, Nixon became the first and only man ever to resign the presidency, on August 9, 1974.

History, like the people who inhabit it, is complicated. While Nixon's tragic, self-defeating chicanery was real, stopping him from attaining a perch as one of America's truly great presidents, his accomplishments are genuine, too. Here was a man who won the geostrategic trifecta: ending direct US combat involvement in the disastrous Vietnam War in 1973; opening a period of détente with the Soviets; presiding over the pivot to China, which ultimately contributed mightily to America's triumph in the Cold War itself, in 1991.

None of these great strategic successes would ever have come about if Nixon and Kissinger had not been dyed-in-the-wool realists. For the opening to China illustrated one of realism's grand strategic precepts. The world is destined to remain anarchic and violent, as it has been since the time of the Trojan War. Given this tragic reality, grounded in the very fiber of human history—there has not been a single day on the planet since the dawn of writing where there has not been a war somewhere—the US must remain eternally vigilant, self-sufficient, and more than adequately armed. But it must do one thing more. It must be ruthlessly prepared to cut deals with less than savory leaders and countries if doing so furthers basic US interests and those of its people.

Dealing with the undoubted monster that was Mao helped the US to win the Cold War, thus securing for future American generations the blessings of liberty, freedom, and a world run on generally favorable US terms. In our own era, we must continue to move away from the Wilsonian fairy tale of simplistic good and evil and instead look good and hard at our still-anarchic planet.

For example, lost in all the self-congratulation about the Biden administration uniting the west against Russia over the Ukraine war, there lurks an underlying disturbing geostrategic reality of our new era: the developing world is not yet prepared to decisively side with either the west or the United States. Over Ukraine, strikingly, nine of the ten most populous countries in the world (India, China, Indonesia, Pakistan, Brazil, Nigeria, Bangladesh, Russia, and Mexico) have been studiously neutral regarding the conflict, or have actively sided with the Kremlin, despite a drumbeat of American pressure. The simple reality is that in the new Sino-American Cold War, developing-world regional powers continue to hedge their bets.

A number of these countries are not democratic, or are imperfect democracies at best. A number have leaders I do not want dating my daughter. None of that means the United States should not do everything in its power over the next generation to win over a majority of these pivotal states, as their support could well spell the difference over time between a Chinese-dominated world and an American-dominated planet. The higher plane of ethical realist morality surely dictates that making future deals with the devil might just ensure an American-dominated world, which morally, for all our country's failings, is infinitely superior to any alternative.

~ 9 ~

THE SHINING CITY
ON A HILL

*Ronald Reagan and the power
of the American example*

The magic of being perpetually underestimated

All of his life, Ronald Reagan was serially underestimated. It became one of his greatest political strengths. To eastern political elites, his sunny, unbridled, sentimental patriotism—which gently allowed that American democracy, for all its flaws, was morally superior to the evils of Soviet communism— seemed to harken back to an earlier, simpler age, before the advent of moral relativism. The smug Wilsonians were right in seeing Reagan as a throw- back, but they, along with the Soviet Politburo, entirely missed the point.

Reagan's easygoing but profound love for his country was not an act. Rather, like a method actor, his "performance" came from deep inside the man and echoed his very essence. It was real, in a way the relativist sophisticates of the time could not begin to fathom. It was real, and it became this formidable leader's greatest weapon.

For Reagan knew something fundamental that the cynical center- left commentariat of his day did not. He understood the great practi- cal power of the American example. The "Great Communicator" saw America as a special place, a shining city on a hill, a beacon of freedom to the rest of the world. There was a reason that Europe's refugee scien- tists had fled to the United States, rather than settling in South America or some far-flung outpost of the British Empire. The United States was a wonderful place to live, free from war, economically dynamic and gener- ally meritocratic, and possessed of a personal and constitutional freedom that was the envy of the world.

Its world-renowned industries used the unparalleled individual freedom of the place to constantly remake itself, as Bill Gates and Steve Jobs were to discover. Its globally emulated movie and entertainment sector was to largely determine worldwide cultural tastes, even as American letters, with seven twentieth-century Nobel Prizes in Literature to its credit by the time of Reagan's presidency (Steinbeck, O'Neill, Faulkner, Hemingway, Lewis, Buck, and Bellow), towered over the rest of the planet.

This made it, and still makes it, a magnet for strivers from around the globe, and endows American foreign policy with the true strength that emanates from the magnetic pull of soft power. This fact, which the relativist sophisticates that so disparaged Reagan's supposed naivete simply could not see, was the guiding light for the whole of the fortieth president's miraculous political rise.

Our ninth realist precept flows from Reagan's wildly successful career, a man who understood better than anyone that the American example to the world is a great source of its global power. One of the country's greatest foreign-policy selling points is the obvious domestic success of its institutions and way of life. In our new era, the US must remain a "shining city on a hill," the showcase for what freedom can bring, rather than being in the foolhardy neoconservative business of trying to impose democracy on the rest of the world at the point of a gun.

Reagan, like the Jeffersonians and Jacksonians of today, understood that this colossal American advantage is perpetually fragile, depending on the continuing world-beating performance of the country relative to the strivings of the rest of the globe. The power of the American example was a real and formidable foreign policy advantage the ordering power enjoyed, but also one that was always up for grabs. As he put it, "Freedom is never more than one generation from extinction."[1]

This was the enduring link between US foreign and domestic policy. An overly promiscuous foreign policy could not help but eat away at

181

America's attractive domestic example of the practical benefits of living in the freest country in the world. As such, a foreign policy that endangered the domestic tranquility and success of the American republic was to be avoided at all costs.

Ideological in his rhetoric about American exceptionalism, Reagan proved to be far more pragmatic in policy terms, precisely because this guiding light of his thinking allowed for the fragility of the American experiment. It is striking that late in his life, after the dementia that characterizes the dread disease of Alzheimer's set in, Reagan still remembered his youthful days as a lifeguard along the Rock River in small-town Illinois, where he had saved an impressive seventy-seven people from possible drowning. In essence, Reagan came to think of himself as the lifeguard for the bedraggled American people.

The Reagan revolution—which restored the innate self-confidence of a country haunted by the tragedies of Vietnam, Watergate, stagflation, the Soviet invasion of Afghanistan, and US haplessness in the face of the Iran hostage crisis—was based on just a few simple ideals. First, Americans had to be freed from the yoke of overmighty, sclerotic, big government. Second, the world had to be freed from the reality and threat of communist oppression, which was patently a more evil system than the American democratic model.

If these were the unalterable strategic goals of the Reagan presidency, in terms of the tactics to achieve them, he and his able first-term governing troika of Edwin Meese (the de facto prime minister), James Baker (head manager), and Michael Deaver (in charge of public relations and the family/dealing with Nancy) could be infinitely flexible.

Ronald Wilson Reagan was born on February 6, 1911, in Tampico, Illinois. His father, Jack, was a shoe salesman, who despite a genuine gift for the gab never quite made it, as his taste for whiskey tended to get in his way. "Dutch," as he was known, was a remote little boy, and remained emotionally distant his entire life, much like FDR hiding his feelings behind an iron cloak of charm and amiability. As the shrewd historian Edmund Morris put it, "Ronald Reagan is a figure of benign remoteness."[2]

On the other hand, Reagan's mother, Nelle, a devout Christian devoted to her son, became the guiding, positive force in Dutch's young life, encouraging his religious upbringing as well as his love of acting and the arts, and urging him to be a perpetual striver. Jack finally curbed his innate wanderlust, settling in Dixon, Illinois, with his family when Dutch was nine.

Dutch did adequately at high school, but excelled in drama, played football, and was a champion swimmer. This latter skill got him the job as lifeguard on the nearby Rock River, where he worked for six summers, ten hours a day, in what would remain his all-time favorite form of employment. His political career was also to be highlighted by the notion of rescue, this time of his down-on-their-luck countrymen from the perils of poisonous despair.

Attending small, nearby Eureka College, Dutch's grades were poor, but he had the lead in most of the college's plays, graduating at the height of the Depression in 1932. Unlike the fortunes of so many, Dutch almost immediately found work, in just six weeks becoming the sportscaster for a local radio station in Davenport and then in Des Moines, Iowa. His signature ability was to vividly call baseball games from a wire report, without actually seeing the game live itself. Reagan's ability to imagine things beyond the present was a potent skill all his life, culminating in imagining a world that did not yet exist, with the extinguishing of Soviet communism.

By 1937, Dutch was on his way to Hollywood. He appeared in more than fifty films, only once playing the villain. Reagan's background was and remains unique in the presidential pantheon, as he became a well-known movie actor who almost ascended to the A-list of Hollywood stars in the 1940s, before a gradual decline in his popularity set in following World War II.

As the president himself understood, his strange background for the highest job in the land became a great political advantage, as he effortlessly made the ceremonial parts of the presidency (a job encompassing British kingly duties as well as practically being the prime minister in policy terms) his forte. As Reagan once wryly quipped, there were times when he wondered how you could actually do the job if you hadn't been an actor.

Starting in the traditional Hollywood guise as a liberal Democrat, Reagan's politics migrated rightward. All his life Dutch liked order and stability, and his visceral reaction to studio strikes (inspired by some far-leftist involvement) dramatically turned him into a fervent anti-communist, even as he ascended to the important position of president of the Screen Actors Guild in 1947–52 and 1959–60. Marrying lifelong soulmate Nancy Davis (his second wife) in 1952, Dutch had a loyal partner to weather his political journey ahead.

They were to be a formidable strategic couple. Where he was likable, positive, and tended to think the best of people, Nancy was utterly devoted, cunning, ruthless, and the family enforcer, who tended to think the worst of people. While he was CEO of their common political destiny, she was the personnel director, vetting prospective staffers as to their suitability to serve the Reagan cause.

Reagan himself was perhaps the most enigmatic figure in American politics since FDR. Kind yet calculating, honest, decent, dutiful, gentle, emotionally self-sufficient, uncomplaining, hardworking if self-centered, he expertly glided through life's surface waters, concealing the depths beneath the waves.

Reagan's movie star decline in the 1950s was righted when he was made the celebrity host of *General Electric Theater*, a highly popular television series of the era, making a handsome $125,000 a year. Appearing every Sunday evening on American television, if anything Reagan's stature in the country rose during the decade. In addition to his hosting duties, Dutch crisscrossed the US for General Electric, giving speeches to its huge workforce, in what amounted to an ideal apprenticeship for his coming life in politics.

Quickly taking on the concerns of GE employees and businessmen over the eight years he was the company's spokesman, Reagan began to talk more about anti-communism and unshackling US industry from an intrusive central government. His political program in place, Dutch was ready to make his unconventional leap into the heart of American politics.

In 1964, Reagan gave a stirring speech, "A Time for Choosing," on the advancement of conservative values, in an effort to help sustain Barry Goldwater's doomed campaign for the presidency. While nothing could buttress the grim, dour, Goldwater, the speech left Reagan a star of the right—the coming man in Republican politics.

By January 1967, Reagan found himself Governor of California, having beaten the formidable incumbent Pat Brown by a whopping 1 million votes in November 1966, 57 to 42 percent. Showing his conservative fangs, Dutch popularly restored order to the perpetually restive campus of Berkeley in 1969 by calling out the National Guard. Easily winning re-election in 1970, Reagan pragmatically tacked to the center in his second term, passing a welfare reform bill by collaborating with the Democratic majority in the California Assembly. Dutch left office in 1975 with the general approval of a majority of Californians, no mean feat in the divisive 1970s.

In 1976, running an insurgent conservative campaign against the incumbent, Gerald Ford, Dutch came within a whisker of the GOP's nomination for the presidency. Tacking to the right of the establishment Ford over foreign affairs, Reagan criticized the president and Henry Kissinger for their policies of détente toward the Soviet Union and for turning over the Panama Canal.

By 1980, after four years of the hapless Jimmy Carter, Reagan's time had at last come, as his signature platform of advocating less government, a stronger national defense, and a restoration of American greatness perfectly met the concerns of the age. Reagan focused much of the campaign attacking the incumbent president over foreign policy, particularly Carter's debilitating passiveness in the face of the Soviet invasion of Afghanistan and the effrontery of the Iranian hostage crisis.

Dutch won a decisive victory over Carter in 1980, triumphing in forty-four states, and taking 489 electoral votes to the Democrats' 49. Ironically, much like his first hero, FDR, Dutch felt he was on a mission to restore America's belief in itself. Here the great power of his fidelity to the American ideal was to play a pivotal role. Reagan became the fortieth president, serving two terms from January 1981 to that same month in 1989. His ultimate monument was that, by the time he left office, the Cold War—which had dominated American strategic thinking since the 1940s—was all but over, and entirely on US terms.

The power of the word: Reviving America

Throughout his presidency, Reagan's rescue of both the country and the world had two prongs: "moral warfare against communism, and continued restoration of the national spirit."[3] For the latter, Reagan masterly used the bully pulpit of the presidency to make a renewed case for American exceptionalism—that the country remain "a shining city on a hill." In terms of foreign policy, he made the case against the Soviets in an unfashionable (in the left-leaning commentariat's eyes) but devastatingly effective moral manner, being unafraid to point out that the Soviet system was clearly more wicked than its western, democratic counterpart and that people everywhere would innately prefer freedom to its totalitarian alternative.

Of course, the Reagan years were peppered with more than their share of concrete historical highlights. First, Reaganomics led to economic deregulation and significant tax cuts, which jump-started the

US economy (while leaving it awash in federal deficits). Second, the White House increased the arms race with the Soviets, hoping to drive their rivals into bankruptcy and concessions at the negotiating table (which dramatically came to pass). Third, early in his term the president heroically survived a serious assassination attempt, emotionally binding him to a large majority of the American public.

Fourth, the Iran–Contra scandal almost derailed this highly successful presidency. Fifth, with the ascension of the reformist Mikhail Gorbachev as the new Soviet leader, an earth-shaking thaw with the USSR emerged that reached its apogee with the INF Treaty, which cut into both countries' stockpiles of nuclear weapons. Sixth, the beginning of the end of the Cold War itself (leading to an American victory) was put into motion.

But for all of these necessary details, it was rhetorical victories over American self-doubt and the evils of totalitarianism (extolling the virtues of freedom) that probably mattered most.

In Reagan's first term he achieved "an overnight resurgence of American patriotism and positivity."[4] He largely did this through the presidential bully pulpit, using rhetoric to restore the country's sagging morale in a way that had not been done since the halcyon days of FDR. But Reagan was working with tropes he had used and fervently believed in, the whole of his career. At last, the moment was ripe for the message.

As far back as his Hollywood days, Dutch had envisioned America as a special place. Reagan gave the oration at the funeral of Staff Sergeant Kazuo Masuda, whose parents had faced wartime internment in California even as their son went on to heroism in defense of the US in World War II. In solemn tones, defending Masuda's sacrifice, Reagan sketched out the country's endless promise: "America stands unique in the world—a country not founded on race, but on a way and an ideal. Not in spite of, but because of our polyglot background, we have had all the strength in the world. That is the American way."[5] America, unlike any other country on the planet, at its best cared not where you came from but in your fealty to the notions of liberty, striving, and advancement.

It was these ideals—and not blood and shared history—that bound the democratic experiment together. Even then, Reagan understood that this made America different and exceptional, a nation of strivers who had come to its shores from around the globe to live free and do better. In the dark days of the early 1980s, this was just what the country yearned to hear—a return to the better angels of its nature. Reagan fervently believed in the greatness of the United States, and his belief and rhetoric were powerfully infectious.

Far from being opportunistic, Reagan's rhetorical credo strikingly did not change during the tumultuous decades that marked his political career. In a 1952 commencement address at William Woods College, he had continued in the same vein: "I, in my own mind, have always thought of America as a place in the divine scheme of things that was set aside as a promised land."[6] Reagan fervently believed in, and expertly communicated, that the country's unique greatness was the result of it being founded on principles, rather than merely being a mistake of history.

As G.K. Chesterton put it, "America is the only nation in the world that is founded on a creed. That creed is set forth with dogmatic and even theological lucidity in the Declaration of Independence."[7] The creed's defining attributes include an attachment to personal liberty not found elsewhere, republican egalitarianism, individualism, populism, and laissez-faire economics. To be an American is to accept a profound ideological commitment, one which Reagan cherished and understood to be without parallel.

But Dutch, much like today's Jacksonians and Jeffersonians, also believed that the American experiment was fragile, and perpetually in peril. During his landmark A Time for Choosing speech of 1964, which made him the conservative standard-bearer almost overnight, Reagan well expressed this contradictory sentiment.

As he starkly put it, the contest between conservatives and progressive technocrats was ultimately about the fate of liberty, "whether we believe in our capacity for self-government or whether we abandon the American Revolution and confess that a little international elite in a far-distant capital can plan our lives better than we can plan them ourselves."[8] Echoing today's Jacksonians, Reagan saw the contest for the preservation of freedom as never-ending. He went on, "If we lose freedom here, there's no place to escape to. This is the last stand on earth."[9]

Rhetorically, Dutch's exceptionalist view came to be associated with the notion of the US as "a shining city on a hill," Puritan leader John Winthrop's trope of the country as an example to the rest of the benighted world. In his concession speech to his campaign staffers in 1976, following his heartbreaking loss to Gerald Ford for the Republican presidential nomination, Reagan had (quite rarely for him) teared up and said, "Don't give up your ideals ... recognize that there are millions and millions of Americans out there who want what you want ... a shining city on a hill."[10]

Winthrop's vision echoed the Gospel of Matthew 5:14, which states, "You are the light of the world. A town built on a hill cannot be hidden." For good or ill, America was to be the world's great experiment in whether free people could effectively govern themselves. As Jacksonians and Jeffersonians today agree the stakes of the American experiment could not be higher, Reagan, in his sunny way, reveled in history's challenge to his country.

The president understood precisely what he was doing. During the 1980 presidential race he made it explicitly clear in saying, "I have quoted John Winthrop's words more than once on the campaign trail this year— for I believe that Americans in 1980 are every bit as committed to that vision of a 'shining city on a hill' as were those long-ago settlers ... These visitors to that city on the Potomac do not come as white or black, red or yellow; they are not Jews or Christians; conservatives or liberals; or

Democrats or Republicans. They are Americans awed by what has gone before, proud of what for them is still ... a shining city on a hill."[11]

Unafraid, for all its tragedies and evils, to say that the arc of American history was a unique, positive accomplishment, Reagan's sunny vision was as inclusive and aspirational—that the work remained not wholly done but a more perfect union awaited the country—as it was inspiring. Linking American history to the country's unique assimilation of hundreds of millions of people, Reagan harnessed the power of the American story, of America as example, believing its fragile majesty must not be squandered.

In his second inaugural, he continued, saying, "Our new beginning is a continuation of that beginning created two centuries ago when, for the first time in history, government, the people said, was not our master. It is our servant; its only power that which we, the people, allow it to have. That system has never failed us."[12] By placing the country's travails in this larger, positive historical context, Reagan underlined the stakes of what was going on, even as he reassured his worried countrymen that America would meet the challenges of their time.

It is striking, and a sign of the idea's importance to him, that Reagan returned to the shining city at the end of his farewell address as president on January 11, 1989. "I've spoken of the shining city all my political life, but I don't know if I ever quite communicated what I saw when I said it. But in my mind it was a tall, proud city built on rocks stronger than oceans, wind-swept, God-blessed, and teeming with people of all kinds living in harmony and peace; a city with free ports that hummed with commerce and creativity. And if there had to be city walls, the walls had doors and the doors were open to anyone with the will and the heart to get there. That is how I saw it, and see it still."[13]

A strong, inclusive, hard-working, prosperous society, built on fidelity to the ideal of liberty. This is what America was to Ronald Reagan and to the millions of Americans he galvanized through rhetoric into believing we could succeed in keeping faith with our revolutionary forebears.

For the president, the power of the American example remained ongoing. He concluded his remarks with a simple, if eloquent, reaffirmation of American exceptionalism. "She's [America's] still a beacon, still a magnet for all who must have freedom, for all the pilgrims from all the lost places who are hurtling through the darkness, toward home."[14] America's magnetic power of example, as Reagan knew, not only keeps faith with all those who have come before us, but serves today as an unquantifiable but profound source of American power.

The most moving testament to Reagan's belief in American exceptionalism came with his farewell to the country. On November 5, 1994, with the scourge of Alzheimer's disease plaguing him, the former president said goodbye to his country, but not without one more written admonition. "In closing, let me thank you, the American people, for giving me the great honor of allowing me to serve as your President. When the Lord calls me home, whenever that may be, I will leave with the greatest love for this country of ours and eternal optimism about its future. I now begin the journey that will lead me into the sunset of my life. I know that for America there will always be a bright dawn ahead."[15]

Far from being ethereal, Reagan knew that—in a continental-sized landmass populated by over 300 million Americans—the only practical way to govern such a huge, cumbersome republic was through the power of rhetoric. Using his formidable ability to connect with the American people, the re-emergence of a confident patriotism was one of the things that Dutch was most proud of regarding his presidency.

And the country overwhelmingly responded. In his triumphant 1984 re-election campaign, Reagan carried an astounding forty-nine states, winning the popular vote by a whopping 59 to 41 percent over Walter Mondale, while dominating the electoral college 525-13. Reagan's command of the bully pulpit and his keeping faith with the unique origins of the American experiment in liberty had restored faith to his hard-pressed people, even as they endowed him with an almost unimaginable political victory.

The power of the word: Defeating totalitarianism

Mikhail Gorbachev, the last leader of the USSR, came to genuinely like Ronald Reagan, staunch anti-communist—such was the charm of the man. The two men were the central characters in four summits between 1985 and 1988, which marked the momentous beginning of the end of the Cold War. For all this, Reagan never wavered in his lifelong goal of ending Soviet communism. To do so, first, he was committed to a massive defense buildup in order to convince the Soviets that—as economically they could not compete—they would be forced to the negotiating table. The plan was to build up military and nuclear forces to then draw them down from a position of American strength and Soviet weakness. It succeeded brilliantly.

Second, and ultimately even more importantly—as Reagan put it to the British parliament—with the weakening of the USSR, "the march of freedom and democracy ... will leave Marxism-Leninism on the ash heap of history."[16] At the time, the western commentariat snidely derided Reagan's vision as naive, and wishful thinking in the extreme. But then again, Reagan had spent a lifetime being underestimated.

Having begun to restore his own country's faltering confidence, Dutch went on the rhetorical offensive, declaring moral war on the Soviet Union, explaining his willingness to bankrupt it by forcing it into military increases its sclerotic and inefficient economy simply could not afford. Moving beyond standard Cold War American strategic doctrine, as his commencement speech at the University of Notre Dame in 1981 made clear, Reagan upended the apple cart saying, "The West won't contain

Communism, it will transcend Communism."[17] The Soviets, in Reagan's view, could ultimately be defeated, not merely negotiated with.

Reagan steadfastly refused to believe the popular postmodern vision that, as all states and people are flawed, they are somehow equal. For all the many grievous mistakes American foreign policy has led the country and the world into, Reagan instinctively knew that it was the center-left western elite's moral relativism, and not his belief in American exceptionalism, that was naive.

A world run by the Kaiser, Imperial Japan, Hitler, Stalin, or Mao (or their heirs) would not have been as just and happy a place as one ordered by the United States. Reagan sunnily refused to follow fashion and bend over this fundamental historical point. In not doing so, he attained great rhetorical power, as communist dissidents in Eastern Europe and Russia did indeed look to America for the better future that Reagan put forth in his speeches, using the US as example.

As Reagan said when challenging nuclear freeze activists, "I urge you to beware the temptation ... to ignore the facts of history and the aggressive impulses of an evil empire, to simply call the arms race a giant misunderstanding and thereby remove yourself from the struggle between right and wrong, good and evil."[18] As Morris perfectly puts it, "in 1983, he had simply and accurately equated totalitarianism with evil."[19] The American example, while far from perfect, was simply better.

The Berlin Wall speech of June 12, 1987 is the classic example of Reagan's rhetoric in action. The highlight of the oration, the president's call—"Mr. Gorbachev, tear down this wall"[20]—was deleted out of the speech's earlier drafts on numerous occasions. Almost the whole of the American foreign policy establishment, aghast at Reagan's bellicosity, wanted the line removed.

The State Department, wrong as so often, fretted that the harsh rhetoric would hamper American efforts to negotiate further nuclear arms reductions with Gorbachev. The West German government worried such a challenge to the status quo in Berlin could lead to instability. The German Foreign Ministry went so far as to urge that speech not be given near the wall at all. Looking back six months later, the left-leaning *Der Spiegel* contemptuously characterized the address as "the work of amateurs."[21]

But Reagan knew better. When the State Department privately assured the president that West Berliners no longer cared about the wall and the communist repression that it symbolized, Reagan's speechwriter, Peter Robinson, reported back to the president after a number of private dinners that, on the contrary, the people of the city still detested all that it stood for. That was enough for Reagan, wary as he was of the west's relativist expert class, which had lost sight of the fact that the American example of liberty was still a potent one.

Standing by the Brandenburg Gate, with Chancellor of West Germany Helmut Kohl in the audience, the president called on Gorbachev to open the wall, which had encircled West Berlin since 1961. He went on to say, "The wall cannot withstand freedom."[22] As Robinson has since explained, "Ronald Reagan could imagine a different kind of world. He could imagine a post-Soviet world. He could see a world without the Berlin Wall. If you put him in a position to give a speech in front of the Berlin Wall, he would feel a certain sense of duty to tell the truth as he saw it."[23]

Buoyed by the American example of the power of freedom, never swayed by the poisonous moral relativism that beset that era (and ours), Reagan knew that his brave words were offering direct comfort to democratic dissidents in Eastern Europe and Russia itself, and that average Europeans still cared a great deal about whether they were free or enslaved by Soviet totalitarianism. He went ahead with the speech, which has retroactively been deemed a turning point in the Cold War.

Reagan's prophetic vision soon came to pass. In 1988–90, that most joyously bewildering of times, the Soviets withdrew from Afghanistan, Lech Wałęsa became president of Poland, and in November 1989 the Berlin Wall fell to the ground. On Christmas Day 1991, Gorbachev dissolved the Soviet Union itself. Reagan's speech, so sniggered at when it was presented, had foreseen where the arc of history was bending.

In November 2019, a large statue of Reagan was unveiled near the site of the speech. But it is the winding-down of the Cold War on freedom's terms that is his true monument. Ronald Reagan died on June 5, 2004, from pneumonia and complications brought on by Alzheimer's. In his steadfast understanding of the power of America as example—both domestically and in terms of foreign affairs—he left behind a far better world than he had inherited.

Preserving a more perfect union

There is a gigantic catch to the magic of using the American example as an effective tool of US foreign policy. The advantage is only as good as the domestic state of the country. Far too often, today's foreign policy blob has cared more about what is going on in faraway places of limited importance to Americans, rather than about America itself. During the fraught days following my opposition to the neoconservative-inspired Iraq War, the one laugh line I could always count on in all my speeches was simply to ask, "Do you want your trillion dollars back?"

Of course, the answer to that question for everyone not plagued by lunacy was "yes." Given an extra trillion dollars, rather than worrying about a third-order priority like Iraq, America could have built many better schools and improved a failing educational system, fixed its roads, begun to balance its books, and improved the state of the union, making the country worthy of being thought of as Reagan's "shining city on a hill." Imposing democracy at the point of a gun, as both the neocons and their Wilsonian hawk allies in the foreign policy establishment advocated, grievously hurt us both at home and abroad.

In terms of foreign affairs, we frittered away our supreme global position on a tertiary interest (while ignoring the rise of peer superpower competitor China), even as we neglected the first-order priority that is the American domestic scene, with the country increasingly unable to solve its myriad problems. Such a country has tragically become less of an example for the world, as its domestic fissures have grown even as the foreign policy blob blithely continues to think that America can do everything abroad, despite an unimaginable $32 trillion federal debt screaming otherwise.

What was true in the 2000s is even more the case today. A tragically underreported opioid crisis killed 109,000 people in 2022 (most from fentanyl), far more than died in the whole of the Vietnam War. Our schools are indoctrinated with a poisonous woke ideology, which lopsidedly points out only the tragedies and failings of American history, but none of its earth-shattering triumphs.

All the while the kids are doing so badly academically that teachers' unions have hit on the ingenious scheme of doing away with testing as it might just expose this terrible reality to already-worried parents, who know their kids simply do not know the basics of how to think and what they need to know to succeed. Our roads, bridges, and airports are decrepit and falling apart. The country is riven with political sclerosis. Our federal, state, and local debt rates beggar description.

All this is demonstrably true, and all this is blithely ignored by the utopian war party that makes up neoconservatives on the right and Wilsonian hawks on the left, who act as if all is well with the country. But of course, they have to ignore the obvious, or realist limits would be placed on their endless, expansionistic ways.

The American example is only as good as America is. Ronald Reagan's monumentally successful use of the American ideal, both at home and abroad, only works if the country itself is in healthy shape, moving toward an ever more perfect union. That is surely not the case at this juncture in our history.

If we are to save America for itself, and the idea of America for the world, every single foreign policy initiative must be judged strictly as to whether it is worth the precious blood and treasure of the country, or whether our wherewithal is better spent dealing with our primary interests at home. Above all, we owe it to Ronald Reagan to live up to actually continuing to be a shining city on a hill, for both America and the rest of the world.

CONCLUSION: ANSWERING LINCOLN'S CALL

A realist foreign policy for our new era

Of course, our realist revival of the Republican Party would have stood no political chance of happening had the Wilsonian/neoconservative follies of the past thirty years not discredited the American foreign policy establishment far and wide. However, following the botched Humanitarian Interventions in Somalia, the Balkans, Haiti, and Libya, the ruinous, seemingly endless nation-building wars of choice fought over Iraq and Afghanistan, a vague, misdirected War on Terror (which ignored the rise of peer superpower competitor China), and the economic collapse brought on by the greed and incompetence of the financial crisis, it is hard to think of another governing class so in need of being shown the door.

When I have been back to Washington in recent years, I am assured by many members of this tarnished elite that—all my recollections to the contrary—they were always with me over the lunacy of the neoconservative adventure in Iraq. Their folly cost over $1 trillion, led to the rise of Iran in the Persian Gulf, the advent of the madness of ISIS, and the deaths of hundreds of thousands, all for absolutely no US strategic gain. I smile wanly and quietly mention that I don't remember their support during the dark days when a fever broke over the land. They look embarrassed and turn away. As they should. But now it is time to right the wrongs of the past generation and do a vital service for an American people who have been so badly led by their self-regarding elite for these many years.

In other words, it is time to answer Lincoln's challenge. We must nobly save (rather than meanly lose) the last best hope of mankind, preserving the American republic by constructing a realist foreign policy fit for purpose to tackle the immense challenges of our new age—leaving the country, and most of all its people, better than we found them.

* * *

By using American history as our guide, such a successful foreign policy can be constructed organically by looking at the lived experience of the citizens of the republic over these past 250 years. For, as we have seen, realism has played a major role in the American foreign policy story since the dawn of the country.

In fact, the three great geostrategic innovations in American foreign policy thinking—Washington and Hamilton's acceptance of the Jay Treaty (leading to American dominance of the North American continent), John Quincy Adams's promulgation of the Monroe Doctrine (leading to American dominance of the Western Hemisphere), and FDR's invention of the Roosevelt Rule, which to this day provides the vital yardstick for when interventions ought to take place (securing America's global advantage)—are all realist in nature.

It is time to remember and rediscover our best selves, as the Jacksonians and Jeffersonians who make up the lion's share of the Republican Party unite for the coming generations over a successful realist foreign policy that is their forgotten birthright. The precepts that follow on from our look at American history are true for all time, but also function as the compass points on today's realist map, determining a successful American foreign policy for our new era.

The Washington/Hamilton collaboration, unbettered in the whole history of the country, provides the first piece of the puzzle. In facing down vociferous opposition and signing the crucial Jay Treaty with Britain, our first administration set the course for nothing less than US domination of North America and permanent great power status. By making it clear that alliances should only be entered into when they advance specific and primary American interests, the founders laid down a realist yardstick that must be rediscovered today.

For instance, even established agreements, including the NATO alliance itself, should only be continued if they are shown to be presently clearly serving American interests. After almost seventy-five years of endlessly waiting for Charlie Brown to kick Lucy's football, it is past time to ask if European countries care about their own security half as much as Americans do. Even with war raging in next-door Ukraine, only seven NATO countries hit the 2 percent spending target in 2022 (with the US, UK, and Poland being the only larger powers to do so).

That leaves fully twenty-three others shamefully free-riding off the US, with countries such as France, Germany, Italy, and Spain cross-subsidizing their ridiculously profligate social spending habits off the backs of the hard-pressed American taxpayer.

Bluntly, as America rightly pivots toward the Indo-Pacific—where much of the world's future growth will come from as well as much of its future political risk—Europe must take charge of its own backyard, in North Africa, the Balkans, and even over dealing with Russia, as America has other things to do in the world. Europe must either put up or shut up. In any event, NATO only matters if European states stop behaving like lotus-eaters, giving Americans actual reciprocal value in terms of our common defense.

Second, John Quincy Adams, the greatest US Secretary of State in the nineteenth century, echoed President Trump in seeing that "No more stupid wars" should be a cornerstone of American realist thinking. Just as Adams skillfully steered the US clear of conflict with Europe over Spain's restive colonies in the New World, with the Monroe Doctrine securing US dominance over time in the Western Hemisphere, so should modern America remember this tried-and-true foreign policy adage.

For the thing that both Wilsonian and neoconservative wars of choice over the past thirty years have in common—besides abject strategic failure and a tragic and colossal waste of America's precious blood and treasure—is that the stakes are so low. Be it Humanitarian Interventions in Haiti and Libya, or nation-building exercises in Iraq and Afghanistan, in absolutely none of these cases were primary US interests in play.

For example, once the American military and intelligence services (quite brilliantly) dislodged al-Qaeda from Afghanistan and routed the Taliban, everything that followed amounted to mission creep. A highly successful initial mission based on the primary American interest of disrupting the murderers of 9/11 gave way to a failed, costly, unwinnable nation-building occupation, with the American-installed government risibly lasting mere days on its own after two decades of support. Frittering away American patrimony for such small stakes must never be allowed to happen again, as the promiscuous foreign-policy establishment never met an intervention it didn't like.

This precept leads seamlessly to the next, the underrated William Seward's notion that American action (or equally importantly, inaction) depends entirely on whether primary US national interests are in play. In the Secretary of State's case, avoiding a needless war with superpower Great Britain was paramount, as this was literally the only way that the Union might actually lose the American Civil War, which was obviously the most important of US interests. Whatever the tactics, Seward focused on avoiding an unnecessary conflict that might just have cost the Lincoln administration everything.

Likewise, today, the benefits of not acting should always be considered, especially in opposition to a feckless foreign policy establishment that responds to the most dangerous of policy phrases, "We have to do something." Often, as Seward deftly shows, America does not. Rather than behaving like a witless fruit fly, driven on by the immediate rather than the important, America should save its fire for the few primary interests that matter. America just about avoided significant involvement in the murderous Syrian civil war, which while heartrending involved absolutely no primary American interests whatsoever.

Serving as genuine stewards of American blood and treasure, our new realist foreign policy involves America actually making choices based on our country's specific interests—actual strategic determinations—rather than just agreeing to do everything, as the present foreign policy blob compulsively calls for. That feckless road leads only to imperial overstretch and the definitive decline of the American republic itself.

Fourth, as Senator William Borah's heroic intellectual duel with Woodrow Wilson makes clear, despite fevered Wilsonian visions regarding the overarching importance of "the international community," American sovereignty is real and everything, be the issue managing America's porous borders, promoting energy independence, or not outsourcing US decision-making to unelected, international technocrats. The agency of the American people must not be infringed, allowing foreign Lilliputians to tie the American Gulliver up.

In the end, despite Wilsonian center-left dreaming, it is the nation-state that continues to drive international relations. A country's agency, its freedom to act as it must to pursue its own national interests, is absolutely vital to running any successful foreign policy. To commit an act of grievous self-harm and outsource decision-making to others is the sign of a country in the process of committing suicide.

For instance, the goal should not be to sign the Kyoto Protocol, or any other international treaty, merely because the rest of the world is determined to agree on a piece of paper many of them will never live up to. Rather, America must only accept international agreements when they clearly serve the primary needs of America—and these interests are articulated precisely by the president to the American people—rather than serving the desires of a global, unelected, center-left commentariat trying to use US power to further their own self-interested ends.

Fifth, it must be accepted that fighting wars is necessary, but only as a last resort for the country. More often than not, America's rivals are Slobodan Milosevic rather than Adolf Hitler—nasty, tinpot dictators rather than revolutionary powers determined to upend the global order in favor of creating a new one. US military action must be rare, only undertaken when the country faces a threat to the established, largely pro-American global order. But given that the stakes would then be the highest, America must fight to win.

From early on, FDR sensed that Hitler (and to a lesser extent the militarists in Japan) posed a threat to the relatively benign global order of his day, and therefore had to be stopped. Over a period of years, he expertly, step by step, moved the American people—then cossetted in a ruinous isolationism—toward this dreadful, if accurate, strategic realization. Roosevelt managed to politically change American public opinion in time to save the world from the dark night of Nazi barbarism, creating the Roosevelt Rule, which to this day provides the essential realist yardstick for when the US ought to militarily intervene in conflicts and when it should not.

Roosevelt's great insight was to remember that geography largely determines geostrategy. The dominant Eurasian landmass, with most of the world's people and resources, stands to dominate the rest of the planet if either its European or Asian portion is controlled by any one great power. America, dominating the peripheral Western Hemisphere off the coast of Eurasia, will continue to be the world-ordering power only as long as neither Europe nor Asia is controlled by any other power.

In this, American geostrategy strikingly echoes that of the last ordering power, Great Britain, whose centuries-old foreign policy involved seeing that no great power came to dominate next-door Europe. As such, London saw off the Sun King, Napoleon, and then the Germans, in order not to have their global dominance upended from the Eurasian landmass (or more precisely, the European end of it).

The rediscovery of the Roosevelt Rule, the great ideational insight of this book, ought to continue to govern American foreign policy to this day. It has massive implications for setting the terms for when and where America must militarily intervene in the world and when it should not, making clear when the US faces a Milosevic and when it faces a Hitler. For example, by FDR's yardstick, the Ukraine war is a sideshow that ought not to ever involve American military intervention, and should only be of limited importance to the country.

Russian president Vladimir Putin, heading a great power in obvious decline, a corrupt gas station with an economy only the size of Italy, cannot even manage to take over Ukraine, let alone threaten a NATO country. While it was right that some aid be given to Kiev to stave off its annihilation in the initial stage of the war, the Roosevelt Rule makes clear that everything beyond this is a strategic overreaction.

Instead, under the Wilsonian Biden administration, the US ruinously pores $110 billion in unaccounted-for dollars into the hands of a corrupt, third-order priority. Suffice it to say, I can hear our enemies laughing at us from here, given that the blob is yet again frittering away the American patrimony for third-order strategic imperatives.

On the other hand, China's threat to dominate Taiwan and the rest of the Indo-Pacific does meet the test of the Roosevelt Rule. This is where the US must absolutely focus its energies, as the region is where most of the world's future economic growth will come from. A China that takes over Taiwan and escapes from the pro-American countries comprising the first island chain strategically hemming it in (Taiwan, Japan, the Philippines, Singapore, Indonesia, Malaysia, and down to India and the Strait of Malacca) can sail its fleet and commercial vessels unhindered out into the blue waters of the Pacific and Indian oceans.

Given its already dominant trading position in the region, this strategic shift in fortune would undoubtedly leave Beijing as the dominant power in first the Indo-Pacific, and over time the whole of Asia itself.

Ultimately, we would come to live in a world dominated by China. In our new Cold War with Beijing, Taiwan is the new Berlin, the strategic canary in the coal mine that informs us as to who holds sway. As long as Taipei is pro-American, so is the region. A dramatic change in its political fortune means that a revolutionary change in the nature of the Indo-Pacific—and over time, the world—has come to pass.

Fortunately for the US, Xi Jinping is not the leader that Deng Xiaoping was. A true radical, impatient with history, Xi's China has scared the horses, throwing an increasingly frightened Indo-Pacific into America's waiting arms. Herein lies the chance for the US to best China without firing a shot.

By aggressing against great power India in the Himalayas, starting a trade war with Australia over their call for a conference to determine the origins of the Covid pandemic, bullying Japan in the East China Sea, bullying everyone else in the South China Sea, overflying Taiwan constantly, stamping out the Hong Kong democracy movement, and oppressing the Uighurs in northwestern China, Xi has unwittingly provided a foretaste of the feast to come of the grim world that Chinese dominance would lead to.

Usefully from an American point of view, the region has responded. Great power Japan has pledged to double its defense spending in the near term, and allows the US the use of bases in Okinawa which can resupply Taipei. Rising power India is increasingly in the American camp in the Indo-Pacific. Under Ferdinand Marcos Jr., the Philippines has pledged to let America use two of its bases in the north of the country, which can also be used to resupply Taiwan.

The Quadrilateral Initiative, comprising superpower America, great powers India and Japan, and Anglosphere partner Australia, has formed a nascent anti-Chinese alliance in the region. Australia, along with the US and UK, has signed the AUKUS treaty, a defense pact which cements the Anglosphere's focus on allying against Beijing's increasing adventurism. All of this limits the window for Beijing to make a dash for Taiwan.

The political risk in the Indo-Pacific is now. If peaking power China—demographically getting old before it gets rich and increasingly friendless in the region—cannot take Taiwan by 2030, it will get harder and harder to practically do so. The danger will pass as Beijing settles for being a superpower and competitor to the US, but one existing in a still-US-dominated world.

To get to this rosy outcome, the US must focus like a laser beam on the region, which is nothing less than the key to the future of our world. America must use geoeconomics to further bind its allies together, even as AUKUS, the Quad, and the Five Eyes (the premier intelligence alliance in the world, comprising Anglosphere countries the UK, Australia, New Zealand, Canada, and the US) work ever more in tandem. Building and constantly diplomatically and politically strengthening its ties in the Indo-Pacific will bolster American deterrence, making a Chinese invasion far less likely.

But in the end, if all else fails and China ruinously commits to force, America—to secure its future, and with primary interests on the line—must be prepared to militarily act. The Roosevelt Rule makes it clear that China in the Indo-Pacific poses the only real threat to primary American interests in the world. To defuse this threat, a realist foreign policy calls for the US to focus intensely on the region, bolstering US deterrence by every means possible to avoid the worst. But if the worst does come to pass, it also makes it clear that America must be prepared to militarily act and to win a war of Chinese aggression over Taiwan.

Sixth, as President Eisenhower made clear, foreign policy is not some game of Risk created for the amusement of the Washington establishment. It exists to secure the betterment of the American people. The Eisenhower administration managed to balance the federal budget an unprecedented three times. It is unsurprising that a foreign policy based on upholding peace led to the prosperity of the 1950s. For in a way that today's foreign policy blob has entirely forgotten, Ike knew that economic strength is the keystone of overall national power, and that the foundation of military strength is always economic strength.

Eisenhower warned against a military-industrial complex, a permanent war party that will always pursue a foreign policy without limits. Ike's nemesis is still around today, as many in the foreign policy elite madly advocate massive US involvement in third-order-priority Ukraine as well as in the Indo-Pacific, as though the country's unimaginable $32 trillion deficit simply does not exist. Eisenhower understood, as only a man who had served in the armed forces for most of his life could, that for many reasons, war must be the last resort of the country, not the first. Among these, economic penury will always lead to the ruination of a country without foreign policy limits.

For every American initiative going forward, a realist foreign policy demands we confront those who refuse to make choices as to what the US should do in the world. Once again, the costs of intervention must be weighed against the good such treasure can do for American society itself. By reinstating this long-forgotten yardstick, America will come to focus, as it should, more on its own country, rather than ruinously overly fretting about tertiary priorities abroad.

Seventh, the experience of John Kennedy during the Cuban Missile Crisis makes it clear that focusing on primary US interests leads to another advantage, as a decision-maker is able to shut out the noise that is the curse of our 24-hour news cycle, concentrating only on the essential.

In clearly articulating that the US had two overarching primary interests in play during the crisis—getting the missiles out of Cuba to restore the global political equilibrium, and avoiding nuclear war—JFK clearly saw facts that eluded hawks such as Curtis LeMay (not overly worried about the dangers of nuclear war) as well as doves like Adlai Stevenson (not overly worried about the dangers of appeasing Khrushchev). This strategic certitude allowed Kennedy to master the missile crisis, as every flexible tactic was weighed in the service of his overriding goals.

Likewise, JFK used his fixed understanding of the primary US interests at play to shut out all the other noise—not letting tertiary events distract him, not allowing the immediate to take the place of the important. When China invaded India during the momentous days of 1962, Kennedy wittily informed his brother he could only deal with one crisis at a time.

This focus was based on JFK correctly making the choice that nothing else in the world then mattered as much as mastering the missile crisis. Rather than doing endless things badly—the present foreign policy establishment lives and dies by laundry lists of what America ought to be doing abroad—JFK did less and did it better, as he focused on the primary things that mattered to his worried countrymen. Presently, the Indo-Pacific meets the "Kennedy test" as to what matters, in a way all the verbiage spilled over the Ukraine war simply does not.

Eighth, a modern realist foreign policy demands that, to further the primary interests of the country, the US must sometimes make deals with the devil. America must reach agreements that further American interests with countries whose leaders I do not want dating my daughter. For, as Richard Nixon's triumphant pivot to China illustrates, foreign policy is not primarily about working with Canada. To secure the country's position in the world, realism demands that US leaders instead treat with countries that advance US interests, even if they fall entirely short of our own Jeffersonian ideals.

In engaging Maoist China, even at the height of the lunacy of the Cultural Revolution, the Nixon administration helped sow the seeds for victory in the Cold War by creating a triangular diplomacy in which both China and the USSR were strategically closer to America than they were to each other. Nixon well knew that Mao was the Charles Manson of international relations, being directly and indirectly responsible for the deaths of literally tens of millions of people. But realism dictated then, as it does now, that we focus on furthering the interests of Americans, precisely because in advancing our own interests we see to it that the world is not run by such monsters.

In the present day, beyond the challenge of the Indo-Pacific, about the only other primary American interest in jeopardy is the worrying fact that many of the emerging regional powers of the world are still studiously neutral over the west's contest with the autocratic powers in Russia and China. If we look further at the more important Sino-American Cold War, much of this rising rest of the world is hedging, determined to side with neither superpower.

These countries must be engaged, based on us finding interests in common that draw us closer together, as for them to fall into the orbit of China would amount to a strategic calamity for the US. Many of these states are imperfect democracies. Many of them have leaders who one would not want to be friends with. But all of them, imperfect as they are, represent an important political force that will play a role in determining the future direction of the world. To disdain them amounts to feeling good rather than doing good. Paradoxically, we must engage those we socially and politically disagree with if the future of the planet is to favor Americans and all we hold dear.

Finally, we must keep faith with the underrated power of America as example, a force the shrewd Ronald Reagan used to great effect in restoring America's confidence in itself as well as in winding down the Cold War on US terms. The catch in the use of this important foreign policy tool is that the power of the American example is only as strong as the actual health of America itself.

A country that has neglected its domestic problems simply cannot be a beacon for the rest of the world. We have suffered through a generation where the foreign policy establishment has seemed to worry about every foreign problem under the sun while concentrating far less on America's own domestic ills, even as trillions were spent abroad on second-order priorities like Iraq.

Presently, the country has a crippling and under-discussed $32 trillion federal debt, a failing education system, creaky roads and infrastructure not worthy of the greatest economy in the world, and an opioid crisis that killed an astonishing 109,000 people last year (more than died in the whole of the Vietnam War).

History teaches us that great powers tend to be destroyed from within, be it through these practical social failings or pernicious self-harming ideologies like the poisonous woke creed, which lopsidedly dwells on American missteps while never bothering to reckon with the great historical triumphs of our country. In either case, the political risk is very much us.

Part of restoring a realist foreign policy to a central place in American thinking is in perfecting the American union, restoring Reagan's potent "shining city on a hill," making the country as example a continuing magnet for the rest of the world as it once was and can be again. To do so, every foreign policy initiative (and I must tell you, I have never heard this idea mentioned even once at my Council on Foreign Relations meetings) must meet an additional test.

As was discussed regarding the Eisenhower example, all foreign policy initiatives must be judged as to whether they are worth the precious blood and treasure they may cost, or whether that money and focus are better spent on making the country "a more perfect union." Just this one major change in the American foreign policy mindset would lead to a renaissance in both foreign and domestic policies.

For it is past time for us to answer Lincoln's eternal challenge. By restoring a realist foreign policy as the governing view of the Jacksonians and Jeffersonians who comprise the Republican Party, we can, over time, remake America. And in doing so, we can remake the world. The plan is here. The rest is up to you.

ACKNOWLEDGMENTS

Writing books is the hardest creative thing I've ever done but also the most rewarding. For books last forever. I would be remiss in not mentioning with the deepest gratitude all the eternal support, friendship, and yes, love, that has made the blessed burden of this project so light.

This wildly ambitious book would never have gotten off the ground without the stalwart and unyielding support of the Stand Together Network, particularly Reid Smith and Hugo Kirk, who have practically and creatively encouraged me to dare more boldly (to coin a phrase) throughout this exciting time. In addition, my friend (both personal and political) Dan Caldwell has always been there to push me onward.

John Gay and the whole of the John Quincy Adams Society have been there for me at every turn. John took time out of his hectic schedule to help me copyedit the book, with the skill of a first-rate public policy intellectual and the selflessness of a friend.

My friend Diane Banks of Northbank Talent Management kindly and crucially pointed us in the right direction regarding finding the right publisher. The book team we have assembled with Whitefox Publishing, led by John Bond and Annabel Wright, has been a perfect fit for our demanding creative and practical needs, never sacrificing quality of the highest order to our beyond-demanding schedule. Whitefox are pioneering a new way for publishing books, and I am certain they will revolutionize an industry badly in need of it. Likewise, in working with our creative and indefatigable publicist, Kathleen Schmidt, I know I am merely part of a creative team of the first order.

People often airily talk about friendship, but Ronald Noble makes the concept an action verb. A close friend, Ron has been an endless champion of our work, and his shrewd kindness and support have been invaluable in seeing this grand project through.

My political risk firm's core creative team has made this project a great joy, and coming to work together has been an adventure I would not have missed for the world. Scarlett Kennedy, my researcher, was thrown in at the deep end, figuring out what her job was on the fly. Against all odds, she triumphed and has been a vital part of the process. I have no doubt she will deservedly have the brightest future.

As anyone who knows me at all is well aware, absolutely nothing would get done—creatively or practically—without my partner in crime and chief of staff, John Goodnight. John, "We few, we happy few, we band of brothers" must have been written by Shakespeare with us in mind. It is an honor and great fun to get to be creative with you every single day. Long may we try to change the republic for the better.

My long-suffering family have had to put up with me thinking about the world at times when I should have been thinking about what is in front of my nose. It has been a journey to find you all, to be with you, but an odyssey worth the world to me. To the five children in my life—Benjamin, Matilda, Samuel, Elisabetta, and Riccardo—you are my personal stake in caring about the future, the practical reason that making the world a more decent place actually matters to me. Know you are loved and valued beyond measure. Samuel, the kids' mini-dedication of the book is for you, and the halcyon days we have spent playing basketball together.

As for the five cats who share my writing days with me (Witch Witchenton—head researcher, Milka, Mandela, George (for Washington), Winston/Tato (for Churchill), thank you for always making me laugh and humanizing me.

Finally, to Sara, the great love of my life. For me, every journey, intellectual or otherwise, begins and ends with you. Thank you for all the quiet things you do, the warmth and the love we all live in because of you, which gives me the space to reach for the stars. May I always be there to hold your hand.

BIBLIOGRAPHY

Adams, F. Charles. "The Trent Affair," *The American History Review*, vol. 17, no. 3 (April 1912), pp. 540–62.

Adams, John Quincy. "Speech to the US House of Representatives on Foreign Policy, July 4, 1821," https://loveman.sdsu.edu/docs/1821secofstateJQAdmas.pdf.

———. *Writings of John Quincy Adams*, Vol. 7 (New York: The Macmillan Company, 1913).

Ashford, Emma. "In Praise of Lesser Evils: Can Realism Repair Foreign Policy?" *Foreign Affairs*, vol. 101, no. 5 (September/October 2022).

Berg, A. Scott. *Wilson* (New York: G.P. Putnam's Sons, 2013).

Black, Conrad. *Franklin Delano Roosevelt: Champion of Freedom* (New York: Public Affairs, 2003).

———. *Richard M. Nixon: A Life in Full* (New York: Public Affairs Books, 2007).

Boller, Paul F. *Presidential Anecdotes* (New York: Oxford University Press, 1996).

Borah, William E. "Against the League of Nations," speech delivered November 19, 1919, https://www.americanrhetoric.com/speeches/williamborahleagueofnations.htm.

Branigan, Tania. "China's Great Famine: the true story," *The Guardian*, January 1, 2013.

Campbell, W.E. "The Trent Affair of 1861," *The Canadian Army Doctrine and Training Bulletin*, vol. 2, no. 4 (Winter 1999).

Cannon, Lou. *President Reagan: The Role of a Lifetime* (New York: Public Affairs, 2000).

Carlson, Cody K. "This week in history: President Wilson offers the Fourteen Points," *Deseret News*, January 8, 2015.

Chernow, Ron. *Washington: A Life* (New York: Penguin Books, 2010).

De Witte, Melissa. "Reagan's 'Mr. Gorbachev tear down this wall' was almost left unsaid, recalls former speechwriter, now Hoover Fellow," *Stanford News*, November 6, 2019.

Donald, David Herbert. *We Are Lincoln Men: Abraham Lincoln and His Friends* (New York: Simon and Schuster, 2003).

Edel, Charles N. *Nation Builder: John Quincy Adams and the Grand Strategy of the Republic* (Cambridge, MA: Harvard University Press, 2014).

Eisenhower, Dwight David. "Farewell Address," January 17, 1961, https://www.archives.gov/milestone-documents/president-dwight-d-eisenhowers-farewell-address/.

Elkins, Stanley, and Eric McKitrick. *The Age of Federalism: The Early American Republic, 1788–1800* (Oxford: Oxford University Press, 1995).

Ellis, Joseph. *Founding Brothers: The Revolutionary Generation* (New York: Vintage Books, 2000).

———. "'John Quincy Adams: Militant Spirit,' by James Traub," *The New York Times*, April 4, 2016.

Fenby, Jonathan. *Modern China: The Fall and Rise of a Great Power* (London: Penguin Group, 2008).

Ferris, Norman B. *Desperate Diplomacy: William H. Seward's Foreign Policy, 1861* (Knoxville, TN: University of Tennessee Press, 1976).

Fisher, Marc. "Tear down this wall: How Reagan's forgotten line became a defining moment," *The Washington Post*, June 12, 2017.

Gach, Margaret. "The Trent Affair," The Water's Edge (blog), November 18, 2021, https://www.cfr.org/blog/twe-remembers-trent-affair.

Glass, Andrew. "Senate spurns the League of Nations, November 19, 1919," Politico, November 19, 2018.

Goodwin, Doris Kearns. *Team of Rivals: The Political Genius of Abraham Lincoln* (New York: Simon and Schuster, 2005).

Hulsman, John. *To Begin the World Over Again: Lawrence of Arabia from Damascus to Baghdad* (New York: Palgrave Macmillan, 2009).

———. *To Dare More Boldly: The Audacious Story of Political Risk* (Princeton: Princeton University Press, 2018).

Isaacson, Walter. *Kissinger: A Biography* (New York: Simon and Schuster, 1992).

Jefferson, Thomas. "First Inaugural Address," March 4, 1801, https://avalon.law.yale.edu/19th_century/jefinau1.asp.

Kaplan, Fred. *John Quincy Adams: American Visionary* (New York: HarperCollins, 2014).

Karnick, S.T. "Ronald Reagan's American Exceptionalism," The Heartland Institute, February 6, 2017, https://heartland.org/opinion/ronald-reagans-american-exceptionalism/.

Kennedy, Robert F. *Thirteen Days: A Memoir of the Cuban Missile Crisis* (New York: W.W. Norton, 1999).

Kissinger, Henry. *Diplomacy* (New York: Simon and Schuster, 1994).

———. *On China* (New York: Penguin Books, 2011).

Kirk, Russell. *The Conservative Mind: From Burke to Eliot* (Washington, D.C.: Regnery Publishing, 2001).

Lieven, Anatol, and John Hulsman. *Ethical Realism: A Vision for America's Role in the World* (New York: Pantheon Books, 2006).

Lincoln, Abraham. "Second Annual Message," December 1, 1862; www.presidency.ucsb.edu/documents/second-annual-message-9.

Lindsey, James M. "The Treaty of Versailles Remembered," The Water's Edge (blog), January 19, 2010, https://www.cfr.org/blog/treaty-versailles-remembered.

Lipset, Seymour M. "American Exceptionalism: A Double-Edged Sword," *The Washington Post*, December 25, 1996.

Luethi, Lorenz M. *The Sino-Soviet Split: Cold War in the Communist World* (Princeton: Princeton University Press, 2008).

MacArthur, Douglas. "Farewell Address to Congress," April 19, 1951.

Maddox, Robert J. *William E. Borah and American Foreign Policy* (Baton Rouge: Louisiana State University Press, 1970).

Mahin, Dean B. *One War at a Time: International Dimensions of the Civil War* (Sterling, VA: Potomac Books, 2000).

McKenna, Marian C. *Borah* (Ann Arbor, MI: The University of Michigan Press, 1961).

Mead, Walter Russell. "Nations Need Leadership, Not a League," *The Wall Street Journal*, November 18, 2019.

———. *Special Providence: American Foreign Policy and How It Changed the World* (New York: Alfred A. Knopf, 2001).

Morgenthau, Hans. *Politics Among Nations: The Struggle for Power and Peace* (New York: Alfred A. Knopf, 1967).

Morris, Edmund. *Dutch: A Memoir of Ronald Reagan* (New York: Modern Library, 1999).

Murray, Rob. "Building a resilient innovation pipeline for the Alliance," *NATO Review*, September 1, 2020.

Naftali, Timothy. "President Nixon's Trip to China: Fifty Years Later," Council on Foreign Relations, February 25, 2022, https://www.cfr.org/event/president-nixons-trip-china-fifty-years-later.

Neustadt, Richard E., and Graham T. Allison. "Afterword," *Thirteen Days: A Memoir of the Cuban Missile Crisis* (New York: W.W. Norton, 1999).

Nevins, Allan. *The War for the Union: The Improvised War 1861–1862*, Vol. 1 (Old Saybrook, CT: Konecky and Konecky, 1971).

Newton, Jim. *Eisenhower: The White House Years* (New York: Doubleday, 2011).

Nichols, Christopher McKnight. *Promise and Peril: America at the Dawn of a Global Age* (Cambridge, MA: Harvard University Press, 2011).

Nixon, Richard M. *The Memoirs of Richard Nixon*, Vol. 2 (New York: Warner Books, 1978).

Parsons, Lynn Hudson. *John Quincy Adams* (Lanham, MD: Rowman and Littlefield Publishers, 1999).

Patterson, James T. *Mr. Republican: A Biography of Robert A. Taft* (Boston: Houghton Mifflin Company, 1972).

Reagan, Ronald. "A Time for Choosing," October 27, 1964, https://www.reaganlibrary.gov/archives/speech/time-choosing-speech.

——. "Farewell Address to the Nation," January 11, 1989, https://www.reaganlibrary.gov/archives/speech/farewell-address-nation.

Remini, V. Robert. *John Quincy Adams* (New York: New York Times Books, 2006).

Schlesinger Jr., Arthur. "Foreword," *Thirteen Days: A Memoir of the Cuban Missile Crisis* (New York: W.W. Norton, 1999).

Sherwin, Martin J. "Inside JFK's Decision-making During the Cuban Missile Crisis," *Time*, October 16, 2020.

Smith, Jean Edward. *Eisenhower: In War and Peace* (New York: Random House, 2013).

——. *FDR* (New York: Random House, 2007).

Stahr, Walter. *Seward: Lincoln's Indispensable Man* (New York: Simon and Schuster, 2012).

Taubman, William. *Khrushchev: The Man and His Era* (New York: W.W. Norton and Company, 2004).

Taylor, John M. *William Henry Seward: Lincoln's Right Hand* (Washington, D.C.: Brassey's, 1991).

"Tear Down This Wall: Ronald Reagan and the End of the Cold War," Bill of Rights Institute, https://billofrightsinstitute.org/essays/tear-down-this-wall-ronald-reagan-and-the-end-of-the-cold-war.

United Press International, "1972 Year in Review," UPI.com, May 5, 2009.

Valone, Stephen J. "'Weakness offers temptation': William H. Seward and the resurrection of the Monroe Doctrine," *Diplomatic History*, vol. 19, no. 4 (Fall 1995).

Van Deusen, Glyndon G. *William Henry Seward* (New York: Oxford University Press, 1967).

Vinson, John C. *William E. Borah and the Outlawry of War* (Athens, GA: University of Georgia Press, 1957).

NOTES

Introduction: Saving the last best hope

1 "Party Divisions of the House of Representatives, 1789 to Present," History, Art & Archives: United States House of Representatives, 2013, history.house.gov/Institution/Party-Divisions/Party-Divisions/.

2 Abraham Lincoln, "Second Annual Message," December 1, 1862, www.presidency.ucsb.edu/documents/second-annual-message-9.

3 See Lincoln, "Second Annual Message."

4 Ibid.

5 Thomas Jefferson, "First Inaugural Address," March 4, 1801, https://avalon.law.yale.edu/19th_century/jefinau1.asp.

6 Lincoln, "Second Annual Message."

7 For an Olympian view of all the major US foreign policy schools of thought, see Walter Russell Mead, *Special Providence: American Foreign Policy and How It Changed the World* (New York: Alfred A. Knopf, 2001).

8 For Mead's complete view of Jacksonianism, see Mead, pp. 218–63.

9 For Mead's complete view of Jeffersonianism, see ibid., pp.174–217.

10 For three different but useful takes on what realism amounts to, see Emma Ashford, "In Praise of Lesser Evils: Can Realism Repair Foreign Policy?" *Foreign Affairs*, vol. 101, no. 5 (September/October 2022); Hans Morgenthau, *Politics Among Nations: The Struggle for Power and Peace* (New York: Alfred A. Knopf, 1967); Anatol Lieven and John Hulsman, *Ethical Realism: A Vision for America's Role in the World* (New York: Pantheon Books, 2006).

1: Washington sets us on our way; "Alliances should only be entered into when they advance specific and primary American interests"

1 See Ron Chernow, *Washington: A Life* (New York: Penguin Books, 2010), p. 729.

2 Ibid., p. 731.

3 Stanley Elkins and Eric McKitrick, *The Age of Federalism: The Early American Republic, 1788–1800* (Oxford: Oxford University Press, 1995), p. 375.

4 Russell Kirk, *The Conservative Mind: From Burke to Eliot* (Washington, D.C.: Regnery Publishing, 2001), p. 81.

5 Joseph J. Ellis, *Founding Brothers: The Revolutionary Generation* (New York: Vintage Books, 2000), pp. 136–7.

6 Ibid.

7 Chernow, *Washington*, p. 743.

8 See Elkins and McKitrick, pp. 489–99.

9 Chernow, p. 756.

10 Ibid.

11 Jean Edward Smith, *Eisenhower: In War and Peace* (New York: Random House, 2013), p. 499.

12 Ibid.

13 Quoted in ibid.

2: John Quincy Adams avoids sea monsters; "No more stupid wars"

1 Joseph J. Ellis, "'John Quincy Adams: Militant Spirit,' by James Traub," *The New York Times*, April 4, 2016.

2 Ibid.

3 John Quincy Adams, *Writings of John Quincy Adams*, Vol. 7 (New York, The Macmillan Company, 1913), p. 488.

4 Charles N. Edel, *Nation Builder: John Quincy Adams and the Grand Strategy of the Republic* (Cambridge, MA: Harvard University Press, 2014), p. 164.

5 Adams, *Writings*, p. 81.

6 Fred Kaplan, *John Quincy Adams: American Visionary* (New York: HarperCollins, 2014), pp. 321–2.

7 Edel, p. 166.

8 John Quincy Adams, "Speech to the US House of Representatives on Foreign Policy, July 4, 1821," https://loveman.sdsu.edu/docs/1821secofstateJQAdmas.pdf.

9 Lynn Hudson Parsons, *John Quincy Adams* (Lanham, MD: Rowman and Littlefield Publishers, 1999), p. 117.

10 Robert V. Remini, *John Quincy Adams* (New York: New York Times Books, 2006), pp. 110–11.

11 Anatol Lieven and John Hulsman, *Ethical Realism: A Vision for America's Role in the World* (New York: Pantheon Books, 2006), p. xi.

12 Hulsman, *To Begin the World Over Again: Lawrence of Arabia from Damascus to Baghdad* (New York: Palgrave Macmillan, 2009), p. 18.

3: Focusing on the essential; William H. Seward navigates the *Trent* Affair

1 John M. Taylor, *William Henry Seward: Lincoln's Right Hand* (Washington, D.C.: Brassey's, 1991), p. 297.

2   Ibid., pp. 83–6.

3   Doris Kearns Goodwin, *Team of Rivals: The Political Genius of Abraham Lincoln* (New York: Simon and Schuster, 2005), p. 192.

4   David Herbert Donald, *We Are Lincoln Men: Abraham Lincoln and His Friends* (New York: Simon and Schuster, 2003), p. 249.

5   Glyndon Van Deusen, *William Henry Seward* (New York: Oxford University Press, 1967), p. 336.

6   Goodwin, p. 364.

7   Ibid., pp. 364–5.

8   Dean B. Mahin, *One War at a Time: International Dimensions of the Civil War* (Sterling, VA: Potomac Books, 2000), p. 59.

9   Allan Nevins, *The War for the Union: The Improvised War 1861–1862*, Vol. 1 (Old Saybrook, CT: Konecky and Konecky, 1971), pp. 387–8.

10 Charles Francis Adams, Jr., "The Trent Affair," *The American History Review*, vol. 17, no. 3 (April 1912), pp. 540–62.

11 W.E. Campbell, "The Trent Affair of 1861," *The Canadian Army Doctrine and Training Bulletin*, vol. 2, no. 4 (Winter 1999), pp. 56–65.

12 Mahin, p. 62.

13 Norman B. Ferris, *Desperate Diplomacy: William H. Seward's Foreign Policy, 1861* (Knoxville, TN: University of Tennessee Press, 1976), p. 184.

14 Mahin, p. 7.

15 Margaret Gach, "The Trent Affair," The Water's Edge [blog], November 18, 2021, https://www.cfr.org/blog/twe-remembers-trent-affair.

16 Stephen J. Valone, "'Weakness offers temptation': William H. Seward and the resurrection of the Monroe Doctrine," *Diplomatic History*, vol. 19, no.4, (Fall 1995), pp. 583–99.

17 Walter Stahr, *Seward: Lincoln's Indispensable Man* (New York: Simon and Schuster, 2012), p. 3.

4: In besting Woodrow Wilson, William Borah reminds us that sovereignty is real and everything

1   Robert J. Maddox, *William E. Borah and American Foreign Policy* (Baton Rouge: Louisiana State University Press, 1970), p. 6.

2   Cody K. Carlson, "This week in history: President Wilson offers the Fourteen Points," *Deseret News*, January 8, 2015.

3   Christopher McKnight Nichols, *Promise and Peril: America at the Dawn of a Global Age* (Cambridge, MA: Harvard University Press, 2011), pp. 249–50.

4   James M. Lindsey, "The Treaty of Versailles Remembered," The Water's Edge (blog), January 19, 2010, https://www.cfr.org/blog/treaty-versailles-remembered.

5   John C. Vinson, *William E. Borah and the Outlawry of War* (Athens, GA: University of Georgia Press, 1957), p. 22.

6   William E. Borah, "Against the League of Nations," speech delivered November 19, 1919, https://www.americanrhetoric.com/speeches/williamborahleagueof nations.htm.

7   Ibid.

8   Maddox, p. 62.

9   A. Scott Berg, *Wilson* (New York: G.P. Putnam's Sons, 2013), p. 612.

10 Andrew Glass, "Senate spurns the League of Nations, November 19, 1919," Politico, November 19, 2018.

11 Walter Russell Mead, "Nations need leadership, not a league," *The Wall Street Journal*, November 18, 2019.

12 Maddox, pp. 69–72.

13 See Paul F. Boller, Jr., *Presidential Anecdotes* (New York: Oxford University Press, 1996), p. 245.

14 Marian C. McKenna, *Borah* (Ann Arbor, MI: The University of Michigan Press, 1961), p. 373.

5: Fighting when it is necessary; Franklin Roosevelt saves the United States from the Nazi peril

1   Conrad Black, *Franklin Delano Roosevelt: Champion of Freedom* (New York: Public Affairs, 2003), p. 555.

2   Jean Edward Smith, *FDR* (New York: Random House, 2007), pp. 485–6.

3   Ibid, p. 486.

4   Black, p. 504.

5   Ibid., p. 564.

6   Ibid., p. 480.

7   Smith, p. 416.

8   Henry Kissinger, *Diplomacy* (New York: Simon and Schuster, 1994), p. 378.

9   Smith, p. 465.

10 Ibid., p. 446.

11 Ibid., p. 453.

12 Ibid., p. 455.

13 Black, p. 577.

14 Ibid.

15 Ibid., p. 503.

16 Ibid., p. 620.

17 Ibid, p. 580.

18 Smith, p. 472.

19 Ibid., p. 456.

20 Black, p. 482.

21 Ibid., p. 668.

22 Ibid., p. 474.

23 Ibid., pp. 474–5.

24 Black, p. 612.
25 Ibid., p. 465.
26 See Chapter 4.
27 Black, p. 533.
28 Ibid., p. 534.
29 Ibid., p. 535.
30 Ibid., pp. 662–3.
31 Ibid., p. 557.
32 Ibid., p. 649.
33 Smith, p. 445.
34 Black, p. 605.
35 Smith, p. 485.
36 Ibid., p. 487.
37 Ibid., p. 489.
38 Black, p. 622.
39 Smith, p. 448.
40 Black, p. 641.
41 Ibid., p. 642.
42 Ibid., p. 574.
43 Ibid., p. 628.
44 Smith, pp. 465–6.
45 Kissinger, p. 392.
46 Ibid., p. 370.
47 Smith, p. 518.
48 Black, p. 667.
49 Ibid., p. 675.
50 John C. Hulsman, *To Dare More Boldly: The Audacious Story of Political Risk* (Princeton: Princeton University Press, 2018), p. 137.
51 Black, p. 669.
52 Ibid., p. 676.
53 Ibid.
54 Ibid., p. 679.
55 Hulsman, p. 134.
56 Ibid., p. 138.
57 Kissinger, p. 393.
58 Hulsman, p. 140.

6: An American foreign policy for Americans; Eisenhower takes on the permanent war establishment

1   See Fred I. Greenstein, *The Hidden-Hand Presidency* (New York: Basic Books, 1982).
2   James T. Patterson, *Mr. Republican: A Biography of Robert A. Taft* (Boston, Houghton Mifflin Company, 1972), pp. 575–8.

3 Douglas MacArthur, "Farewell Address to Congress," April 19, 1951.

4 Greenstein, p. 52.

5 Dwight David Eisenhower, "Farewell Address," January 17, 1961, https://www.archives.gov/milestone-documents/president-dwight-d-eisenhowers-farewell-address.

6 Jim Newton, *Eisenhower: The White House Years* (New York: Doubleday, 2011), p. 261.

7 Jean Edward Smith, *Eisenhower in War and Peace* (New York: Random House, 2013), p. 450.

8 Newton, p. 131.

9 Rob Murray, "Building a resilient innovation pipeline for the Alliance," *NATO Review*, September 1, 2020.

10 For a fine account of the genesis of Ike's thinking on the Farewell Address, see Smith, especially p. 760.

7: Defending the primary interests of America; In the Cuban Missile Crisis, JFK shuts out the noise and saves the world

1 Richard E. Neustadt and Graham T. Allison, "Afterword," in Robert F. Kennedy, *Thirteen Days: A Memoir of the Cuban Missile Crisis* (New York: W.W. Norton and Company, 1999), p. 102.

2 We now know the Soviets had four times the number of troops the CIA estimated were in Cuba at the time (fully 43,000), as well as nine operational tactical nuclear weapons in place to repel a US invasion. Fatalities from a nuclear war occurring then were estimated at an incomprehensible 100 million. See Martin J. Sherwin, "Inside JFK's decisionmaking during the Cuban Missile Crisis," *Time*, October 16, 2020.

3 Arthur Schlesinger, Jr., "Foreword," in *Thirteen Days*, pp. 10–11.

4 Robert Kennedy, *Thirteen Days*, p. 26.

5 Neustadt and Allison, *Thirteen Days*, p. 119.

6 Sherwin.

7 Ibid.

8 Neustadt and Allison, p. 120.

9 Sherwin.

10 Neustadt and Allison, p. 108.

11 See Sherwin.

12 Kennedy, p. 98.

13 Ibid., p. 95.

14 Schlesinger, p. 13.

15 Ibid., p.12.

16 Sherwin.

17 Neustadt and Allison, p. 122.

18 Kennedy, p. 37.

19 Ibid., p. 69.

20 Kennedy, p. 82.
21 Hulsman, p. 227.
22 William Taubman, *Khrushchev: The Man and His Era* (New York: W.W. Norton and Company, 2004), p. 579.
23 See Robert Dallek, *John F. Kennedy: An Unfinished Life* (London: Penguin Books, 2004).
24 Kennedy, p. 84.

8: Dealing with the devil; Nixon's pivot to China is the game changer in the Cold War

1 Jonathan Fenby, *The Penguin History of Modern China: The Fall and Rise of a Great Power* (London: Penguin Group, 2008), p. 351.
2 Walter Isaacson, *Kissinger: A Biography* (New York: Simon and Schuster, 1992), p. 335.
3 Ibid., pp. 335–6.
4 Ibid., p. 349.
5 Timothy Naftali, "President Nixon's Trip to China: Fifty Years Later," Council on Foreign Relations, February 25, 2022, https://www.cfr.org/event/president-nixons-trip-china-fifty-years-later.
6 Tania Branigan, "China's Great Famine: The true story," *The Guardian*, January 1, 2013.
7 Lorenz M. Lüthi, *The Sino-Soviet Split: Cold War in the Communist World* (Princeton: Princeton University Press), p. 6.
8 Christopher Andrew, *For the President's Eyes Only: Secret Intelligence and the American Presidency from Washington to Bush* (New York: HarperCollins, 1995), p. 384.
9 Isaacson, p. 343.
10 Ibid., p. 333.
11 Ibid., p. 402.
12 Henry Kissinger, *On China* (New York: Penguin Books, 2011), p. 280.
13 Isaacson, p. 346.
14 Ibid., p. 353.
15 Ibid., p. 334.
16 Richard M. Nixon, *The Memoirs of Richard Nixon, Vol. 2* (New York: Warner Books, 1978), p. 29.
17 Conrad Black, *Richard M. Nixon: A Life in Full* (New York: Public Affairs Books, 2007), pp. 780–2.
18 United Press International, "1972 Year in Review," UPI.com, May 5, 2009.
19 Isaacson, p. 333.
20 Ibid.
21 Ibid., p. 352.

9: The shining city on a hill; Ronald Reagan and the power of the American example

1   Edmund Morris, *Dutch: A Memoir of Ronald Reagan* (New York: Modern Library, 1999), p. 308.
2   Ibid., p. vi.
3   Ibid., p. 581.
4   Ibid., pp. 3–4.
5   Ibid., p. 228.
6   S.T. Karnick, "Ronald Reagan's American Exceptionalism," The Heartland Institute, February 6, 2017, https://heartland.org/opinion/ronald-reagans-american-exceptionalism/.
7   Seymour M. Lipset, "American exceptionalism: A double-edged sword," *The Washington Post*, December 25, 1996.
8   Karnick.
9   Ronald Reagan, "A Time for Choosing," October 27, 1964, https://www.reaganlibrary.gov/archives/speech/time-choosing-speech.
10 Morris, p. 401.
11 See Karnick.
12 Morris, p. 511.
13 Reagan, "Farewell Address to the Nation," January 11, 1989, https://www.reaganlibrary.gov/archives/speech/farewell-address-nation.
14 Karnick.
15 Morris, p. 666.
16 Lou Cannon, *President Reagan: The Role of a Lifetime* (New York: Public Affairs, 2000), pp. 271–72.
17 "Tear Down This Wall: Ronald Reagan and the End of the Cold War," Bill of Rights Institute, https://billofrightsinstitute.org/essays/tear-down-this-wall-ronald-reagan-and-the-end-of-the-cold-war.
18 Morris, p. 473.
19 Ibid., p. 658.
20 Marc Fisher, "Tear down this wall: How Reagan's forgotten line became a defining moment," *The Washington Post*, June 12, 2017.
21 Ibid.
22 See Bill of Rights Institute.
23 Melissa De Witte, "Reagan's 'Mr. Gorbachev tear down this wall' was almost left unsaid, recalls former speechwriter, now Hoover Fellow," *Stanford News*, November 6, 2019.